Journeying Within Transcendence

A Jungian Perspective on the Gospel of John

Diarmuid McGann

Paulist Press ◊ New York ◊ Mahwah

Library of Congress Cataloging-in-Publication Data

McGann, Diarmuid.
    Journeying within transcendence.

    Bibliography: p.
    1. Bible. N.T. John—Criticism, interpretation, etc. I. Title.
BS2615.2.M352 1988 226'.506 87-32756
ISBN 0-8091-2952-3 (pbk.)

Published by Paulist Press
997 Macarthur Boulevard
Mahwah, New Jersey 07430

Printed and bound in the
United States of America

Contents

Introduction:
From Mark to John

The Christian community has traditionally applied the symbols contained in Ezekiel's vision (Ez 10:14) to the four evangelists. It has been suggested that these symbols, of the young man, the lion, the ox, and the eagle, have been ascribed to the evangelists on the basis of where they first have us meet Christ in their respective gospels. To Matthew therefore is applied the young man since Matthew presents us with the human genealogy of Christ,[1] showing him to us as son of David, son of Abraham, etc. Matthew in short presents Christ to us in a human context. By contrast Mark presents Christ to us in the opening scenes of his gospel as one who has spent forty days in the desert and comes striding from it with a message about repentance. For Mark the desert is the place of the beasts, and Jesus went there to battle with them while angels ministered to him.[2] The lion is the proud beast of the desert, the stalking animal of the wilderness, whose symbol best characterizes Mark's gospel. With Luke we meet all the opening characters, and Christ as well, in the temple.[3] It is there that Christ goes to open the scriptures and announce his mission to be the compassionate presence of God who would proclaim liberty to captives, sight to the blind, etc. It was appropriate to designate him with the ox, the animal associated with the temple.

John's gospel presents Christ to us first of all as dwelling with God.[4] He opens his gospel in the soaring heights of the Godhead, in the time before time, in the mystery at the center of God. He brings us right away to the freedom of God himself, whose ways are not our ways, and who wishes to reveal himself to his creation. He presents Jesus to us as that Word which, coming from God, reveals God because he is God. John brings us immediately to the heights and depths of this Jesus, to his transcendence and immanence, to his freedom and commitment, to his divinity and humanity. It is because of this that the eagle, who soars in the sky and is so much the animal of freedom, is the symbol that designates John's gospel. It is a symbol that Brown suggests is largely determined by the "celestial flights of the opening lines of the gospel."[5]

If John's "Christ" and his gospel is designated by the eagle, it seems best to convey John himself by another symbol, the symphonic conductor. John is more than a spectator watching the Christ. He is himself caught up, attracted, transformed, called out, by the vision he sees. He is neither a philosopher nor a theologian of this moment but rather a witness, a proclaimer. He stands like a Bernstein before the notes of his composition, and the instruments of the orchestra are ready to allow the music to come alive in him. He is ready also to shape and share it with others so that they too might have life, that they too might see, and hear, and enjoy. The prologue (vv. 1–18) is his overture. It is a great hymn filled with poetry and rhythm. It develops in strength and tone, in color and intensity, as it moves from its opening in the heavens until it reaches the earth. In it John is sounding all the great themes and notes that shall reverberate throughout the gospel. Each theme is sounded in this hymn, or prologue, and then magnificently isolated, highlighted, and developed in the body of the gospel, until it is blended back into the fullness of the symphony again at the end. It reminds me of the unfolding of a piece like Ravel's Bolero in the hands of Bernstein.

The centerpiece of this gospel is Christ. It is on him that John, even in the prologue, focuses his attention. John sees him not just as music about God but rather as the very music of God. In Eliot's words "he is the music while the music lasts."[6] He presents him to us as the Word of God who becomes incarnate, takes flesh with us and among us, dwells in our midst, is rejected by many, is accepted by a few, and becomes life for them. So central is he for John that he is present in nearly every scene in the gospel as the key figure and central character. Culpepper[7] calls him the "protagonist," and most of the other characters in the gospel he terms "ficelles" by which he means "typical characters who serve specific plot functions." Jesus, for John, is at the center, and so, as the gospel evolves, everyone else is responding or reacting to him (Nicodemus coming to him, the Jews questioning him, the disciples following him, etc.).

John presents Jesus in all five time zones of the gospel: "the pre-historical past, the historical past, the narrative present, the historical future and the eschatological future."[8] He is present in all of them. Initially he is perceived as the eternal Word who is with God in the beginning (cf. Prologue), then he is the expressive Word who is with God at the center of creation (opening chapters), then he is the incarnate Word who is at the center of a spiralling and evolving universal (body of gospel), and in the closing chapters he is the glorious and victorious Word returning through the paschal mystery to the Father.

John is then as we see him a conductor of this great

music that is Christ. Nils Dahl says he is the "ecclesiastical editor of the tradition of the Johannine school."[9] Who was listening to this music? For whom was it written? What was their situation? Current exegesis is constantly exploring these questions and finding out, little by little, more in the way of answers. Louis Martyn put forward the thesis that the gospel was written for a community of people that was in conflict with the synagogue[10] and this thesis was confirmed by the study of Severino Pancaro who has shown extensively that it was written in response to the expulsion of Jewish Christians from their synagogues and the subsequent condemnation of Christians as heretics.[11] Jerome Neygrey has written a very readable and exciting work showing how the "diverse Christological portraits of this gospel grew and developed vis-à-vis the changing experience in the group's history."[12] We will see something of the importance of these works during the course of exploration but refer people to the above mentioned works for an in-depth study of the question of audience, place and situation of composition, etc. We take it that current scholarship indicates a situation that involved both Jews and new Christians together with a large number of people who can best be described as Jewish Christians.

How then do I approach this gospel? Certainly not as an exegete but more as a man who has tried to make it the fountain for my prayer life for these past few years. In the early days of my priesthood I spent most of my prayer time reflecting on the words of the prologue "the Word was made flesh." Then I moved away into what at the time I considered the more fleshly gospels. Now having completed a first trip through each of them over the past twenty years I find myself coming back via the dark journey of Mark to the strength and depth of John. I have basically followed the path I found helpful in praying Mark and that

I outlined in *The Journeying Self*.[13] Essentially it consists in trying to read the gospel not only as a story of Jesus but as my story in and through the story of Jesus. The deep metaphors and symbols of the gospel, the deepest of all being Jesus himself, summon me to prayer, to meditation, to musing and to wondering, to living within the transcendent. The result is this work. It is therefore my attempt at prayer, to live at the point of intersection where the mystery of Jesus meets the mystery of my life and the revelation of God in Christ reveals to me the mystery and wonder of my own being. I have in the process drawn heavily upon the work of C. G. Jung but for the sake of brevity I have refrained from quoting him at length or from referring to his works at every turn in the road.

The written portion of my journeying in its typed form would never have been possible without the presence of Darcy Upton. As with my previous work she has once again voluntarily undertaken the difficult task of reading and translating my penmanship, and, even more than that, she has proved a tremendous asset to me in her response to, and encouragement of, the work involved in writing this book. To her my heartfelt and appreciative thanks.

Chapter 1
John 1:1—1:18
Prologue

John begins his gospel with a prologue. It is perhaps
one of the best known prologues in all of literature. We
shall follow him, although it is perhaps not the best place
to begin from the point of view of prayer. This is so because
it is so dense, so full, so compact that it can be almost too
much as one begins. It is also a very controversial piece of
writing. Exegetes propose different ways of approaching it,
different responses to where John got his basic idea and to
how he shaped it, etc. I shall avoid a deep discussion of this
and accept the proposal put forward by Brown[1] and
Schnackenburg[2] that it is a cultic hymn.

It is best, says Schnackenburg,[3] to distinguish three sections, and he proposes them as follows:

verses 1–5	the pre-existent being of the logos
verses 6–13	the coming of the logos to the world of men
verses 14–18	the meaning of the incarnation for the salvation of believers

6

Within these three sections the prologue portrays for us the life of God as personal and interpersonal, as between Father and Son. It shows us this life as coming among us as life, light and truth. It portrays the graciousness of God as gift, as freedom, and as call, and it shows the goal of life in terms of orientation, direction and judgment. It is little wonder then that it has been considered a masterpiece, a concise statement of the totality of the gospel, an overture that leads us into the full symphony. I shall follow the structure I have outlined above in the remarks which follow.

Verses 1–5. John is a deliberate writer and focuses Jesus in a special way. The way he presents him to us already makes a statement. Paul, for instance, sees Jesus as the Son of God from the moment of the resurrection. Mark in contrast has the centurion make the profession of faith at the crucifixion. Luke sees him as the Son of God from the beginning of his life and casts him as such in the infancy narrative, and Matthew goes even further back than that, tracing his lineage back to the beginning of time. From the beginning he was the Son of God.

John goes one step further, to the beginning of the beginning, to the time before time. It is here that he wishes to begin his journey. Here he tells us that "in the beginning was the Word" (Logos). We are used to hearing words. We know what they are. Even in scripture we have holy words. We can distinguish in our ordinary language different kinds of words, harsh words, romantic, forbidding, commanding, etc. In scripture we have special kinds of words too, covenanting words, wisdom words, historical words, etc. In fact in scripture the word becomes something you can see; it becomes an image for faith. The word has a certain visibility and sacramentality, e.g. the word of creation is an image of life out of chaos and into union, the psalter is an image of man encountering God in sorrow, pain, joy, etc. Is this what John means when he says in the beginning was the word? Yes and no, or, better still, partially. John is not saying that God has put his word into something, a book, a person like the prophets, a movie, etc. It's something stronger than that and much more important. In fact nowhere in the gospel do we read that the word of the Lord came to Jesus and this is because he is God's Word who was with him in the beginning.

This is not an easy thing to grasp. Perhaps another way of approaching it will be helpful. John Tauler[4] says that the Word is the silence of God fully expressed. The Word is who God is when he gets out of himself while remaining within. The Word therefore reveals who God is; in the Word God expresses himself. Furthermore the Word perfectly reveals and fully expresses God because he is the Son. This point is essential to John and it is to it that he will return many times in the gospel. He tells us that "he who sees the Son sees the Father," that "no one knows the Son except the Father and no one knows the Father except the Son and those to whom he wishes to reveal him," that "he who hears the Son hears the Father, for I and the Father are one." In fact at the last supper this appears to be his joy, for he says that he has made known the Father and he will continue to make him known, and he does that through being himself. Culpepper sums it up well when he says, "The revelation of the Father seems to be the distinctive Johannine contribution which has been imposed on the traditional interpretation of Jesus' role in taking away sin."[5]

The opening strophe is not only a vision of the Word, however; it is also a vision of the emergence of creation. John, deliberately in Brown's view,[6] structures the opening verses of the prologue to parallel the opening chapter of Genesis. Now the Word creates, and this means that the world, or, better still, creation, is an act of revelation. But if John says that the Word participates in creation he nevertheless leaves out the "how." He only says that "through him all things come into being and apart from him nothing came to be." He leaves the how for the later speculation of theology.

Theologians have not been slow to speculate. Throughout history many of them have offered their understanding to the Christian community. Meister Eckhart was one such man. He followed the lead of Thomas Aquinas[7] and sees that all of creation, including human persons, is an act of God's creative imagination. Creation, he says, is instantaneous since from the divine perspective God does not act under the constraints of time. This of course does not rule out evolution from a human perspective, but that is not our immediate concern here. For Eckhart, then, all of creation is good. His commentator Matthew Fox says, "It is good, it is gift giving, it is itself a blessing from God. Creatures, all of them, are a divine blessing and a word from God. . . . Divinity dwells on the inside and we can keep God on the outside by being too little in touch with the inside."[8] If God is within, then, he says, we need to get to know the within. It is then that we will be able to "announce the Word, pronounce it, produce it, and give birth to it."[9] Eckhart's reflection and speculation brings us home to the depths hidden in the opening strophe of John's hymn.

Verses 6–13. John keeps his eyes fixed on the Word. In the second strophe he sees the Word as the "bearer of life." He points out throughout the gospel that this is his reason for coming. He comes that we may have life and have it to the full, that his joy may be our joy and that our joy may be complete. He is careful throughout the gospel to say that this offer of life is now, in this moment. Whenever he speaks of life he uses the present tense as if to underscore the importance of the message. The life that Jesus is, the life that he brings, is not just a future possibility, but an experience and a possession right now.

This offer of life "now" is important for John. For him it is true in all phases whether he is speaking of its birth in us (chapter three) or its development (chapter four) or its increase (chapter five) or its nourishment (chapter six). It is true whether he is speaking of how it can be lost by indecision (chapters seven and eight), or how it can be restored (chapters eight and nine), or how it can overcome pain, suffering and death (chapter eleven). It is even true when he is speaking of how it is lived out in love (chapters thirteen to twenty). In all of these times the life that Jesus is, is a current possibility, a now experience. The Word for John is the source of life in all situations and its principle of development.

For John Jesus is not just a life-bearer; he is life. What he gives to us is what he is in himself. The life he gives to us tends toward a definite goal which he will articulate in greater depth throughout the gospel. Basically it boils down to union with him and he speaks of it intensely during the last supper under the image of the vine and the branches.

John goes even further. He says that this life, this Word emerging out of the Godhead, is light for man. He is the true light that enlightens every man. Here he is calling upon a biblical tradition. When God manifested himself to Moses at Sinai he was surrounded by fire and flame and a dazzling light; when he guided the people through the desert it was again as a flame that he presented himself; when the people were in difficulty it was for the light of God's face that they searched. This is the tradition that John draws upon now. The biblical tradition says that God guides his people, illu-

minates their minds and hearts and leads them forward.
Here now John says three things of the Word as light. First
of all he will "cause division, secondly he will cause condemnation of the false life, thirdly he will issue an invitation to come to authentic life, to wholeness and
completeness."[10]

For John the Word reveals the world. Through him it
takes on a certain meaning; he illuminates it. Without him
the world is perceived only peripherally and in an exterior
way. Now however the Word lights up all creation; it lights
up the inwardness of all that is and so he reveals to people
who they really are. He reveals to me who I really am.
Darkness for people is their not receiving the light—the
light which illuminates not their intelligence first but the
heart. When this happens, that is when they are in darkness; then John says that they do not really know who they
are. Light however differentiates; when it is received it illuminates them and then they become aware of who they
really are. The Word does this; it teaches them who they
really are and who God really is. We will see this battle
between the light and the darkness grow, develop, intensify
and be resolved in the gospel.

Verses 14–18. The third strophe speaks of the implications
of the coming of this Word. It cannot be cut off from what
has gone before, so we have already witnessed some of it.
Now John deals with it more specifically. He tells us that
"the Word became flesh; he made his dwelling among us
and we have seen his glory. . . . Of his fullness we have all
had a share, love flowing upon love." He is again appealing
to his history. Both Ezekiel[11] and Joel[12] had said that God
would dwell among his people. He had lived among them.
He had lived with them in the law, being present to them
in the Torah, etc., but the fullness of his presence had not

been present. Sinai was a great event, but for John it was only a preparation. The law was a great presence but for John it is only a shadow. Now the fullness is here. Moses, if you will, had a mystical moment, an intuition, a flash, a passing glance, a glimpse of God passing by, but now in Jesus we have the full revelation of God to gaze upon. He has come this revelation of God among us in the flesh and he has taken up residence among us.

John's vision throughout the prologue becomes mine now in prayer. It helps me to see all of creation as emerging out of God, and this means that I too have emerged out of God. I know that there are many changes that mark each day in my existence, but there is also something about me that is a unique expression of God. Paul says that I am a mystery hidden with Christ in God. John says more—that I am a revelation emerging out of God with Christ. John brings me before the wonder of all creation, a creation that Teilhard de Chardin began to understand when he wrote: "By means of all created things the divine assails us, penetrates us and molds us. We imagined it as distant and inaccessible, whereas we live steeped in its burning layers. *In eo vivimus*, as Jacob said awakening from his dream. The world, this palpable world which we were wont to treat with boredom and disrespect, with which we habitually regard places with no sacred association for us, is in truth a holy place and we did not know it."[13]

The world for Teilhard, like creation for John, is a diaphanous epiphanic milieu alive with the presence of God. But this means that I too am alive with the presence of God. The way to enter it then is not so much the way I have attempted in the past by plunging into the mystery (intellectually conceived) of God but by descending into the midst of humanity, by discovering within me a willingness to be a human among humans. Thomas Merton says that there is "only one problem in which all my existence, my peace, and my happiness depend: to discover myself in discovering God. If I find him, I will find myself, and if I find my true self, I will find him."[14]

As I reflect therefore on the prologue I find myself coming home to the mystery of my own existence. I stand before the Word and recognize him at once as both stranger and friend, as both the Christ I know and don't know. With him I approach my own life wherein he dwells, wherein he has chosen to dwell and to pitch his tent. I acknowledge, or at least I am trying to accept, that I am an emergence out of God. There is a something, or a someone at the center of my life that is somehow an element of the pleroma; there is within me a passionate movement, an impulse, a longing that tends toward what Teilhard called "Christ Omega." I accept my creation not only as a push from behind but as an attraction from the Creator ahead and the movement of the Creator within. I accept what John points me toward in the prologue and that it is true of my life, that I am on a journey under providence toward meaning, intelligence, and love and that the process of my life is awakening to that journey. I accept that my journey in life is a journey within transcendence.

I look to this hymn and it brings me to the hymn of my own life, to the realization that I have my own subjectivity that is itself revelational. I have my own being, my own interior, my own selfness with its own numinosity, and I must reverence it. Secondly, it makes me aware again that all else that is created also has its own subjectivity, its own numinosity, its own revelational quality, and that I must equally stand in reverence before that sacredness. The very earth itself has its subjectivity and now it presses itself upon us. Thomas Berry[15] has written that there exists a certain sequence of major cultural-spiritual phases, a sequence of

codings that may be identified as: (1) tribal-shamanic culture, (2) the great classical religious culture, (3) the scientific
technological culture, and now (4) the emerging ecological
culture. In this new age he feels that we must return again
to "a sense of the earth as matrix of the human, as primary
revelation of the divine, as educator, healer, ruler, as primary commercial enterprise, as primary norm of all human
values and activities." This would be, I feel, to discover
again the path to glory illustrated and revealed in the vision
of John's prologue.

John invites me to my own humanity. He also makes
it clear that there are present forces within me that want to
live in darkness, that do not want to accept the blessing,
that want to live in partiality, in incompleteness, at the border of existence. There are forces that do not want to accept
the subjectivity of life, the revelational nature of all existence, the call to wholeness and totality, etc. For now, however, the gospel question phrased to my being is: "Do I
accept and believe in God's rootedness in me or not?" To
this I answer yes, and so claim for myself in prayer the good
news I see proclaimed in the Word who is from the beginning and who became flesh and dwelt among us.

Chapter 2
John 1:19—2:1
From Call to Mission

When John finishes the prologue he leads us into the body of the gospel itself which Raymond Brown[1] suggests may be divided into The Book of Signs (Chapters 1:19—12:50) and The Book of Glory (Chapters 13:1—20:31). The Book of Signs, as we shall see shortly, relates seven wondrous events, or sign events, that Jesus worked. These events will form the larger part of our reflection. The Book of Glory describes the passion, death and resurrection of Jesus as the process of glorification whereby Jesus returns to the Father. However before John enters into either the first sign event or The Book of Glory, he dwells for a moment on the call of the disciples, and on John the Baptist who is perhaps the major figure of the opening chapter.

Who is John the Baptist? How does he function in this gospel? What is his relationship to Christ? These are important questions for John. He sees the Baptist quite differently from the way the synoptic gospels see him. He nuances his description of him accordingly. The evangelist's purpose, it appears, is to show "Jesus' coming forth from concealment with the help of the divinely inspired testimony of John, introducing himself to his first disciples as the promised Messiah, surpassing and intensifying their hopes, and finally beginning the revelation of his glory with his first sign."[2] In the synoptics John is presented as a rather ascetical figure living in the desert, calling people to repentance and to reform in view of the calamity that is coming their way. His message therefore is: Repent, reform, change your lives, make a path in the desert, prepare the way. His voice has a harsh, demanding tone.

In John's gospel the Baptist is not as fearsome a character. In the prologue he is quite clearly distinguished from the Christ. He is not the light, and when he appears on the scene he reiterates that assessment of his importance. He is not the Messiah, he is not the prophet. The word he chooses for himself is "a voice." That is the category he feels he best fits within. He is essentially for John a witness, a testimony. The prologue had already said, "He came to bear witness, to give testimony to the light," and now we see that happening in the opening chapter.

Since the Baptist's function is to witness to Jesus, John now separates him from all subsidiary functions. He presents the Baptist as the one who sees the dove descending on Jesus and remaining with him. It is the Baptist and not the heavenly voice that announces the event. It is the Baptist who proclaims Jesus. It is the Baptist who on three occasions gives witness to Jesus—first before the envoys who come from Jerusalem, then before the Israelites, and finally before his own disciples and followers. John is so careful to present the Baptist as a witness that he does not have him even baptize Jesus. He does baptize others but not Jesus, and when he is questioned about the meaning of his own baptism he moves the attention away from himself to the one who is greater, who comes after him, the strap of whose sandal he is unworthy to fasten (1:26).

The Baptist is a solid witness. He does not want the limelight. He realizes that he is not himself the center and core. He is not the depth but he tells the people: "There is one among you whom you do not recognize . . . the one who is to come after me." He gives this one a special name when he sees him. He calls him the "lamb," a name with many biblical associations as Raymond Brown points out.[3] The title combines the idea of (a) the lamb of sacrifice, (b) the lamb of the suffering servant of the Isaiah poems, (c) the lamb of final victory. The Baptist in using this title is referring to Christ as all of these. He is the sacrifice, the servant and the victor. As a sacrificial lamb he will be responsible for leading the people from bondage. As the servant lamb he will bear the suffering of his people as he leads them out of captivity. He will serve the community. As the victor lamb he is the guarantee that goodness and wholeness will win out in any battle with evil or partialness. Robert Kysar sums up the lamb's role by saying that he is the "agent of God whose life and death results in liberation. . . . The lamb of God is the liberating revealer of God . . . to know him is to be freed."[4] John points to this lamb and gives witness to him.

Not only is the Baptist a witness who proclaims the presence of the lamb but he is a witness who serves the lamb. There is no competition and no jealousy between them. In fact aside from the beloved disciple the Baptist is the only disciple in the gospel who has no "deficiency in his faith."[5] His loyalty is clearly shown in v. 35 when he separates himself from all those who have been his followers. He distances from them so that they will be freed to follow the lamb. His efforts then are directed toward forming links between his disciples and Jesus. When this has been effected the Baptist fades into the background as the perfect witness who perceived the greatness of Jesus. His work is done and we do not hear from him again throughout the gospel.

It is interesting to note how effective the Baptist's work was because now it begins to form a pattern in the gospel. All the disciples who come to Jesus will come because someone else brings them. Initially it was the Baptist handing over two of his disciples. Only one of these is named— Andrew. It has, however, been traditional to name the other one John, the son of Zebedee, the disciple Jesus loved, but this has never been fully established with certainty by exegetes.[6] Andrew, we are told, then brings Simon. Possibly John brings James. Philip brings Nathanael, etc. In fact Paul Minear makes the following observation: "All the followers of Jesus depend for faith on someone who is not the light. According to the prologue all who believe come to faith through John the Baptist. . . . It is quite typical of this gospel that each disciple should be enlisted not by Jesus directly but by another witness."[7] One clear exception to that is Philip, and we shall speak of him in a moment. For the moment by way of review let us acknowledge the Baptist as important, as witness, as handing over his followers to Jesus and then as fading into the background. With that the focus now turns to Jesus and what he does.

The first thing that strikes me as I look at Jesus in these days before Cana is his question. He asks all those who come to him what they want, which is at once a very simple and profound question. It is not always easy to answer, and in fact in chapter five we will meet a man whose inability to answer the question leaves him paralyzed. This question is meant to probe their deepest longing. It is also an invitation to them to express their needs. Jesus' first question is not that of a judge but is that of a host. His call is a grace, an invitation, a gift. Throughout the gospel this is made clear over and over again. At any time one can refuse the gift, and indeed John points out that some did. In the prologue we are told that "his own did not accept him," and later on, in chapter six, after the story of the multiplication, John says, "Many no more walked with him." The gift can be refused. Nothing is forced on people; nothing is made to happen to them against their will. Jesus respects their freedom and their choice and their capacity to know what they need. The call he extends to them is therefore essentially non-violent, although the hearing of it may involve one in a great deal of pain, suffering and death.

The disciples hear that call; they feel his basic interest in them. At least their response indicates a certain level of comfort with him. They tell him that they wish to know where he lives. Jesus could have responded with an address in Jerusalem or Bethany or somewhere like that, but he doesn't. He seems to suspect that their question has a deeper intent. He sees in their question a desire to know what are the values, experiences, and thoughts that shape his life, and it is to this level of the question that he chooses to respond when he invites them to come and see. We have an expression, "I know where you're coming from," that catches, I think, the direction of their interest. Jesus is inviting them to experience where he "comes from." The burden of the rest of the gospel is to show them what he values, sees and feels, so that in the end they too can come to live where he lives.

The answer given to the disciples' question therefore is not given just once in the gospel. It is given many times. It is a progressive answer that in part depends on the changes taking place within those invited. It becomes evident that they must meet with Jesus, and then they will learn to see as they stay with him. One by one we come across in this gospel people who are brought to Jesus by others, but they come to faith and see only after meeting him. John's disciples are convinced, that is, they see, only when they meet with Jesus. Nathanael is skeptical until he meets with Jesus. Then he is enabled to withdraw his projections and prejudices and discover that good things do come from Nazareth. He learns to see. The community from the Samaritan village learn for themselves when they meet him. Martha professes her faith, Thomas' doubt is transformed, and Peter's love released only in the fruitfulness of the meeting that follows his running away. It is in short necessary to meet with him, and it is in the meeting that people, places and things get changed. Water becomes wine, Peter becomes the rock, bread becomes his body, the dead become alive, the lost are found and the blind come to see.

The answer to the disciples' question is given many times, and people grow in their capacity to see where Jesus lives once they have met him. They learn to see what Jesus sees, and what Jesus sees is the Father. Where Jesus lives is where the Father lives and it is to this that Jesus invites them, to be where the Father is. The full elaboration of this "invitation/answer" is given by John in the second half of the gospel, in The Book of Glory, but it is already hinted at here. Jesus is inviting them into his space so that they can see with his eyes, and when they can do that, then they are empowered and enabled to say, "We have found the Messiah." Eventually in The Book of Glory this invitation to see gives way to abiding in Jesus and indwelling in the Trinity. This is really what seeing is all about.

Philip, as we mentioned, is the one apostle whom John does not mention as being brought by someone else to Jesus in these opening days. Jesus himself appears to call him. What is even more interesting is that he is not called to see but to follow. It is interesting therefore to notice that at the last supper Philip undergoes something of a crisis and that it specifically has to do with vision. Jesus is telling the disciples that he must leave them but that they should not be upset when Philip says to him, "Lord, show us the Father (Let us see, in some translations) and that will be good enough for us." In response Jesus says to Philip, "Have I been with you all this time, Philip, and you still do not know me? To have seen me is to have seen the Father" (14:9). Philip had really missed the whole point. He had difficulty with an incarnate God.

I turn now to these pre-Cana days in my prayer life and try to understand them in terms of a story of self. I recognize within me some of the tension and difficulty that they are pointing toward. These symbols, and people, are part of me. I recognize that I must proclaim the self that is within even though as yet I have not seen. How does one proclaim and testify to the presence of what one has not yet seen? There is an old saying which states that "that which is worth doing is worth doing badly," by which we mean imperfectly. I recognize an aspect of my life that is like that of John the Baptist, that at least wants to point to the presence of the self within me and say that there is the lamb that is servant, and sacrifice, and victor. There is the greater within me breaking into my life. What is John the Baptist doing in these days but scrutinizing all that comes before him, being attentive to whatever comes his way out of the unknown so that when he sees Jesus he recognizes him as the one who "ranks ahead" of him. Regardless of how inconvenient or difficult that task is for him, he attends to it and risks the proclamation. He brings to consciousness and awareness the existence among them, in their midst, of the lamb of God.

The John the Baptist within me senses the Christ in those moments when, while touching my limits, I am nevertheless drawn beyond them. I sense it in those moments when I am in contact with what I might call the transrational as opposed to the irrational; when I am called, invited, drawn out beyond what this frail ego, this rational executive that calculates my life and my vulnerability (in what Eliot would call "spoonfuls,") reaches its maximum point of endurance, and yet I can go a little further. In those moments I discover a deeper self within me that I want to testify to and that I want to surrender my whole being to forever. To this deeper self I want to give all my limitations and all my restrictions, all my followers, that they too will see, and yet I am powerless before that deeper self. It comes to me as gift, as grace, as invitation. Sometimes it appears not to be there at all, and then it comes again out of the unknown and I am aware, I am conscious, I am a witness to its presence. Elizabeth Bowden Howes catches something of my sense of the way things are when she says, "The self is lost to sight in infancy or early childhood and has to be achieved again in maturity. When the self is discovered or touched or more firmly achieved, the ego then works with the self as its faithful servant and knows that it is thereby serving an inner manifestation of the larger purpose."[8] Perhaps in this way I too will learn to see and even to find fulfilled in my life in the days that lie ahead the promise made to Nathanael, "You will see greater things than this. . . . You will see heaven open and God's angels going up and coming down on the Son of Man" (1:50).

Chapter 3
John 2:1—2:12
From Water to Wine

Most adult Christians I know have heard of a place called Cana. It doesn't come as a total surprise to them, bringing a kind of blank stare to their eyes. It may be that they are familiar with the name because it has been mentioned in so many homilies and sermons they have heard or because they themselves have participated in a pre-marital program that bears the same name or indeed for any number of other reasons. In confirmation of that I can tell of a group I was with recently that I asked to associate with the word Cana. Two responses seemed to dominate; one group associated the word with marriage, the second group associated it with the miracle of water being changed into wine.

For me Cana is a place of change but not just any change. It is a place of transformative change. As I read the story in John's gospel, that seems to be the thing that catches my attention. It does not catch me just once but many times as the story unfolds. Initially it is the change of

water into wine. This can best be perceived against the Old
Testament background where wine is connected with the
final days. Its presence is associated with blessing and
favor; its absence is seen to designate calamity, disapproval
and rejection. We read in Deuteronomy, for instance, that
God will punish his people, and the nature of the punishment is shown to be that there will be no wine for them.
He says to them, "Though you plant and cultivate vine-
yards you will not drink or store up the wine, for the grubs
will eat the vine clean" (Dt 28:39). On the other hand Isaiah
gives a different picture that reflects favor and abundance
when he says that "on this mountain the Lord of Hosts will
provide for all people a feast of rich food and choice wines,
juicy rich food and pure choice wines" (Is 25:b).

A second change worthy of note that happens within
the story and that is immediately discernible is between
Jesus and Mary. The dialogue between them is initially at
least a little bewildering. What is the meaning of Mary's
comment to Jesus that "they have no wine"? Was she
merely relating a fact? Was she asking him to do something? Was she mandating something? Was she just
expressing her helplessness at the situation? Different interpretations are given by exegetes. Then there is Jesus' reply
which appears equally confusing. What is the significance
of his words to her when he said, "Woman, how does this
concern of yours involve me? My hour has not yet come"?
Was this response of Jesus a "put-down"? A denial of her
role in his life? A temporary refusal to act as she suggested?
From the many interpretations available, Crossan[1] appears
to me to be on the right track. He notes in the dialogue the
presence of a "Semitic idiom which has to be translated and
understood in the light of the Old Testament." He concludes on the basis of that "idiomatic expression" (what to

me and to you) that Jesus is in fact denying Mary a presumed relationship of unity between them. Rosemary
Haughton[2] in a similar line of thinking draws our attention
to the fact that Jesus is rejecting Mary's request that he act
a messianic part. She believes that Jesus reached here a
point of separation from his mother. He separates himself
strongly and clearly from any simple identification with her
wishes and ideas. In that differentiation they were, she
says, able to discover each other newly and beautifully.
Cana thus is a change from a previous and less mature relationship to a current and more mature one. In terms of Fritz
Kunkel's[3] psychology we might term it the emergence of
the greater we relationship out of the lesser "we." Jesus is
individuating, claiming his own life and the right to follow
his own destiny.

Cana illustrates a third transformative kind of change
in the manner in which it refers to time. Jesus' response to
Mary is that his "hour" has not yet come. What is this hour
and what does it refer to? The word is a technical word for
John which he uses on twenty-six occasions in the gospel.
It can hardly be an accident. For John the "hour" of Jesus is
in the hands of the Father and it refers to the moment of his
passion and death. This is the moment when he accom-
plishes the work given him to do and returns in glory to the
Father. It was, as he tells us himself, for this hour that he
had come into the world and so he looked to it rather than
away from it. The Greeks had two words for time that
might better help us understand. The word *chronos* was a
word they used to designate time as a series of successive
moments. It is the normal meaning we have in mind when
we ask someone what time it is. They generally answer
twelve noon, or three-thirty, etc., specifying a particular
moment in that chronology. The Greeks also used the word

kairos to speak of time. This refers more to the purpose and meaning of time itself. It answers the question "What is time for?" It seems to me that the word "hour" that John uses has more the flavor of this second meaning of *kairos*. From this point on the cross marks his life, and indeed in nearly every chapter John will refer in some way to the cross.[4] Time is not just a succession of moments but rather a meaningful direction of moments. Time is meaningful and each second participates in that meaning. *Chronos* thus is transformed into *kairos* even as *kairos* fills every moment of Jesus' chronological existence.

These three major changes that take place at Cana are not however the only ones. There are others which are important to notice. They almost appear to happen without anybody noticing them and yet they are very much part of the story. Consider for instance the bride and groom. The story indicates that they undergo a change from being a maiden and a bachelor to being a married couple, and if they fade into the background as the story proceeds it is nonetheless true that the convenant transformation they entered was a major one. Here too our eyes turn to the hosts of the party who invite people to come and celebrate with them. They end up being the guests while Jesus, one of their guests, ends up being the host through the "miraculous" event that took place. By his action the story intimates that the party was able to continue so that in a true sense one can say the wedding party is transformed into the Jesus party. Here another change is perceived in that "the precious wine of the gospel is contrasted with the water of the Jewish rites of purification, the order of grace with the order of law."[5] The religion of the old dispensation with its ceremonial laws and rites of purification gives way to the new religion of Jesus.

Cana therefore is for me a place of change. John himself stresses its importance as the place in which "Jesus performed the first of his signs. Here he revealed his glory and his disciples believed in him" (v. 11). As if to underscore the importance of these "signs" he returns to his emphasis at the end of the gospel when he states the value of the signs, "Now Jesus did many other signs in the presence of his disciples which are not written in this book, but these are written that you may believe that Jesus is the Christ, the Son of God" (20:30). In fact John, according to biblical exegetes, records seven such signs in his gospel. They are the Cana story (2:1–11), the healing of the royal official's son (4:46–54), the healing of the paralyzed man (5:1–9), the walking on water (6:16–21), the miracle of the loaves (6:1–14), the healing of the blind man (9:1–41), and the raising of Lazarus (11:1–44). John calls these signs not because they all involve changes similar to Cana but because they point to something deeper. A sign, says Schillebeeckx, is an important work of Jesus, performed in the sight of the apostles, miracles in fact which of their nature lead to faith in Jesus, the Son of God.[6] Signs therefore are Christological in character. They catch the attention of the viewer or reader and focus it on Jesus.

The fact that these signs/events are important for John does not necessarily mean that people will always see through the sign. In fact quite the contrary is true. Many times people seem to miss them altogether and we have a very good example of that in the story of the multiplication of the loaves when so many followed him only because of the great miracle they had witnessed. The sign both reveals and hides. It reveals God's glory to those who believe, but it hides this glory from those who do not—so that Raymond Brown says that signs "have an enigmatic element which divides the audience. Some are prompted by the gift of faith to penetrate the enigma and to come to the revelation behind the sign or the parable; others cling blindly to an exclusively materialistic understanding."[7]

It is not enough, then, just to say that there were changes at Cana. The question is deeper: Did they see the sign in the midst of the change? Remember how after feeding the multitude Jesus again encounters the crowd in chapter 6 and says to them, "I know you have come looking for me because your hunger was satisfied with the loaves you ate, not because you saw signs" (6:26). To see in terms of one's own advantage is not enough. To follow Jesus simply for the sake of the benefits he gives, whether it is healing, or food, or a good party, is not sufficient. One must go beyond that to grasp something of the identity of Jesus himself. If signs are perceived only in their ability to make people gasp with awe and wonder, then in fact they remain inadequate and ineffective.

At Cana John carefully organizes his story of the changes and the awesome deed of changing water into wine so that three groups at least can be identified as being present. The first of these we can describe as "onlookers." They are comprised in large measure of the large number of guests at the party; they are what we might call the general public. From the story they appear to be totally unaware of anything unusual happening. They do not know that there is an insufficiency of wine; they do not perceive the dwindling supply and in consequence of this we can also presume that they are unaware of any miracle occurring. The most they may be aware of is the change occurring in the bride and groom. A second group is present that we can term the staff. They are the chief steward, the waiters and a few servants. They, by reason of their function and position, are obviously in touch with the crisis as it develops. In the story they function as witnesses at a second level. They become aware of the miraculous change of water into wine. They tell of what happened and report it as a fact and as a powerful event. They see the change therefore in terms of power, self-interest, material gain, etc. The third group who are present we can in a general way call "apostles." They are also in touch with the crisis. In fact one of them, Mary his mother, is the one who first of all calls attention to the matter by saying, "They have no wine."[8] They also are aware of the miraculous change from water into wine but they go beyond that to the person of Jesus himself. For them the real or ultimate value of the change that has taken place lies in the presence of Jesus as the incarnation of God's love. They have made the journey, in fact the pilgrimage, from power to love.

As I come to this story now in prayer I am invited to ask: Where is Cana in my life? Where in my life are the transformative changes going on? How do I perceive them and what are they saying to me of the inner deeper self? Do the changes reveal to me that I am living in time as *chronos* or *kairos*? Are the changes only surface transitions in my life or are they revelatory? Is my time merely sequential or purposive? Do the changes truly speak of a process of separation and individuation so that I am coming to both a knowledge of and a possession of my deepest self in a conscious manner? Is my life, in the words of Shakespeare, shown by these changes to be a "tale told by an idiot full of sound and fury signifying nothing," or do they reflect a meaningful whole and completeness emerging at the center of my being?

As I read the story I must admit that my attention is captured by the change from water to wine, and it is caught in such a way that it reveals to me an underlying desire in my life. I am attracted by the power of the miracle, by Jesus' capacity and ability to do that thing. That is what holds my attention, and it is at that level that the story catches me and

I find a desire to be like Jesus in that manner. The story catches me at the level of my power complex without passing me through to the deeper level and insight beyond. But this in itself is helpful, for it brings into awareness and consciousness that which until now has been unconscious. It reveals to me in the outer world Christ the wonder worker, the existence of a *theos aner* Christology,[9] and in the inner world that factor in my own psyche that is sometimes referred to as the "black magician"[10] that strives and drives for control and exhibits extreme grandiosity.

Marie Louise Von Franz[11] says that on the level of animals there are two basic tendencies which to a certain extent contradict each other, the sexual drive and the drive toward self-preservation. In people they appear as two divine and contradictory drives—love and power—love including sexuality, and power including self-preservation. She tells us that the power drive sometimes imprisons the love drive by pretending that it owns it. For me now Cana is discovering that area in my life both in terms of my imprisoning powers and my imprisoned love. To discover the first is to begin to perceive the second; it would in fact be to go from the miracle as event to the miracle as sign. It would be to discover what in fact the story points to—that Cana is where power is transformed into love.

Chapter 4
John 2:12—3:1
From Secular to Sacred

My friend Ginger is a cat who now spends most of the time sleeping or dreaming or whatever it is cats do when they curl up by the fireplace. Now it takes either an earthquake or the mighty pangs of hunger to move him. However it was not always that way. When he was a kitten things were different. Then the slightest movement would catch his attention and cause him to spring into action. Sometimes it was only the moving shadows of the trees that would fire him; other times it was the presence of some real, or indeed imagined, stranger that set him off on his hunt. Ginger knew the importance of movement and was attuned to it. Perhaps it was from him that I learned to watch the subtle changes that indicate the presence of movement. It is not surprising, therefore, that as we turn to John's next story on the cleansing of the temple the thing that catches my attention is movement. Jesus is going somewhere. John heralds this with the announcement of the Passover. There are three such feasts in the gospel of John. Schnackenburg[1] gives them the names "The Pre-Synoptic Passover" (2:13), "The Passover of the Multiplication" (6:4) and "The Passover of the Crucifixion" (11:55). They are all times of movement. The feast itself commemorates the movement of the people out of bondage, and the movement of God to protect and save his people. It was a time when people also were involved in actual physical movement.

It was customary for those who could do so to leave their homes on these occasions and go to Jerusalem to celebrate the feast. In fact for many it became a pilgrimage more than just a journey. Roger Corless points out the difference between the two in that he says pilgrimages are journeys "to a sacred center . . . a journey to the center of meaning. . . . It must be done slowly, recollectedly, savoring the sense of occasion; and its movement is both outward and inward at the same time."[2] During these pilgrimages the people often sang songs as a way of encouraging each other, praying, passing time perhaps, etc. Some of these songs have been preserved for us in the psalms of ascent or degrees (Pss 120–135), which are so called because they depict stages on the journey. Stephen Kaung[3] has written a commentary on these psalms in which he shows how in Psalm 120 the pilgrim begins with an awareness of his existential situation. He discovers himself to be in Mosoch (a town to the north of Palestine) and in Keder (a town to the south of Palestine) at the same time, and out of this there comes the realization that the one place he is not living in is Jerusalem, the center of Palestine. He therefore undertakes a pilgrimage to go to Jerusalem.

What was so important about Jerusalem? Why was it that this was the place to be on these occasions? Why does Jesus appear there? Even in our time there is for the Jewish people something very special about Jerusalem. It is a place that is reverenced and venerated by them. They speak of it with pride and dignity. In the scriptures to be in Jerusalem or on the way to it was the cause of immense joy as we read, "I rejoiced when they said to me, 'We will go to the house of the Lord,' and now we have set foot within your walls, O Jerusalem" (Ps 122). On the other hand, to be away from Jerusalem, to be unable to get there, to be denied the freedom to go there, has always been both for Russian Jews now and for Babylonian Jews in the past the cause of immense sorrow and even depression as we read, "By the streams of Babylon we sat and wept when we remembered you, O Zion. . . . How could we sing a song of God in a foreign land?" (Ps 137).

From one perspective Jerusalem was no different from many other cities of the Near East. Ever since the time of the Sumerian culture in Mesopotamia these cities were the basic social and political unit. I have pointed out in a previous work[4] how many cities were frequently the bearers of feminine names. Many of them in fact were seen as mother cities and the towns close by were referred to as her daughters. These cities were the center of action where things were constantly happening. They were seen therefore in many ways as wombs of life and people gathered there to celebrate life. On the other hand, when one journeyed to a city it was perceived as moving toward a center of order. Thus you have different locations mentioned in relation to the city and they reflect different grades of chaos and order. The desert is uncultivated and uncultured, the place where chaos abounds, a wasteland and wilderness inhabited by the beasts. As one moved from here they came across farmlands and fields which were plowed and in which different crops, etc., were sown. This reflects some cultivation, some civilization, some touch of the human hand and mind. Then there were the suburbs where people met and intermingled, were opened to different ideas and thoughts, different ways of ordering the chaos. At the city center there was city hall where kings governed and the gods were worshiped. Cities therefore, Jerusalem included, are both a womb of life and a center of order and government. Indeed in Jungian terminology we could say that the city is both feminine and masculine.

Jerusalem has its own specific history also in the scriptures which is very interesting and varied.[5] When first we meet it, Melchizedech is its king and it is known simply as Salem, meaning peace.[6] Even then it is described as being unusual. It is a city that reverenced God in the midst of seven other nations or tribes that had no fear or respect for God. Melchizedech extends hospitality to Abraham who was tired after his battle with the four kings and offers him bread and wine and blesses him. Even then Salem was a place noted for peace, tranquility and hospitality. But Jerusalem was also a center for hostility and violence and destruction. It is the place that killed the prophets. One of the scenes in the gospels that is filled with pathos is in Matthew where Jesus is seen to weep over the city and cry out, "Jerusalem, Jerusalem, murderess of the prophets and stoner of those who were sent to you. How often have I yearned to gather your children as a mother bird gathers her young under her wings but you refused me!"[7] Jerusalem is thus at once the place of hospitality and hostility, of peace and destruction, of life and death.

In another set of images that emerges from scripture we see her portrayed metaphorically. Ezekiel in two memorable sermons[8] speaks of her negatively as a harlot and a whore. He reminds her of her origins and that she was the offspring and product of an Amorite father and a Hittite mother on whom nobody looked with favor or compassion. However, Ezekiel says that Yahweh looked upon her and took her in and covered up her nakedness. Anderson comments on Ezekiel, "Yahweh took pity on this illegitimate child whom others rejected, nurtured her to the beauty of full maidenhood and plighted to her his troth. . . . But the maiden trusted in her own beauty, forgetting that she owed her life and her beauty to God. . . . She lavished her harlotries on any passer-by, for her lust was a wild wanton power within her like that of her passionate Hittite mother."[9] Jerusalem thus is the unfaithful harlot. On the other hand John, standing on the island of Patmos, sees her quite differently as the book of Revelation comes to a close. He sees "a new Jerusalem, the Holy City, coming down out of heaven from God, beautiful as a bride prepared to meet her husband, and I heard a voice cry out . . . This is God's dwelling place among men."[10] This is a vision of Jerusalem as the virgin bride now coming to her lover, not in infidelity but in faithfulness.

Jerusalem itself is built on two hills and surrounded by many others. One of these hills housed the temple, the sacred dwelling in which God lived among his people. On the other hill lived those who served the temple, such as Caiaphas the high priest, but who had grown rich on the gifts of the poor. This was the source of power. From this particular vector then, Jerusalem is at once the place of the sacred and the secular, the holy and the profane. What then is Jerusalem with its two hills, this center of government and center of worship, this city of kings and city of gods, this masculine center of order and feminine womb of life, this place of hostility and hospitality, this place that is both virgin bride and harlot whore? It is the place of opposites, and it is to this place on the great feast of Passover that Jesus now moves to celebrate the liberation of his people and their destiny.

On entering the city he goes to the temple which must not be perceived as being like our churches. It is a large and complex area. In what is known as the outer court the merchants sold sheep, doves and oxen. These were then taken by the purchasers to the inner area where they were used in sacrifice. At the time there were two kinds of coinage in use. One of these was Roman and bore the image of pagan gods. It was considered not acceptable currency in the temple so that banks or centers of monetary exchange were established within this outer court. It is this area that Jesus enters. All four evangelists mention this event, which thereby stresses its importance. They disagree as to when Jesus entered here. In general the synoptics place the event that occurs now as taking place just before Jesus' trial, passion and death. John places it at the very start of his ministry. Both groups are utilizing this to their own theological advantage. What happens is more important to us.

Jesus, according to John, "makes a whip." This is not an impulsive action. There is deliberation here. Then he puts the buyers and sellers out of commission. The point here, as Huckle indicates, is not "that there were abuses going on in the temple. . . . Judaism would have been a unique religion if there were not. . . . Jesus drives all the elements of the cult out of the temple, making the normal sacrifice impossible."[11] That is the point, and the authorities are aware of it, for they ask him for a sign that indicates he has authority to do that, to bring an end to the temple sacrifice and worship. Jesus' response that if they "destroy this temple in three days he will rebuild it" is seen by Brown as an "eschatological proclamation referring to the Jerusalem temple" and that the "insight that it referred to the body of Jesus was a post-resurrectional amplification."[12] In either case, however, it appears that Jesus is clearly following up on what was said at Cana and indicating that the old order was passing away and a new order was beginning.

This concept of replacing the temple and the old way

of life continues all through the gospel. John portrays Jesus as replacing—some will prefer the word fulfilling—everything that was connected to anything else that was important in the Old Testament. He does this in a systematic way. First he presents the great leaders and teachers of Israel, men like Moses, Abraham, Jacob, and Isaiah, men who were supposed to have seen what no one saw—God. John now disputes that claim and says they did not see God. What they saw was Jesus.[13] Jesus, however, does see God, and therefore he is superior to either teachers or prophets. Second, he takes all the life-giving symbols of the Old Testament—the lamb of sacrifice, the well of Jacob, the desert manna—and he will show that Jesus is the fulfillment of all of these in supporting, sustaining and nourishing his people. Finally, he brings the great feasts of the Old Testament forward and shows Jesus as replacing the water and light, the central symbols of the feast of Tabernacles, and then he finally presents him as the lamb of Passover who is killed on the same day, at the same hour, and in the same manner (with unbroken legs) as the Passover lamb. John therefore has Jesus not just once but consistently replacing the temple throughout the gospel so that people will soon come to worship the Father neither "on this mountain nor in Jerusalem but in spirit and in truth" (4:22).

The question for us now is to discover what this all looks like in our life. How do we understand it as a story of self? What is Jerusalem and what is the temple that must be cleansed, purified, replaced, etc.? Jesus as we have been perceiving him is the self within leading us now to that place of opposites in us. It is a place that frequently we do not want to touch. Jung speaks of the opposites of the conscious and the unconscious which stand in a complementary relationship to each other. In fact illness is what happens when we isolate in one area alone. Neurosis is living consciously but without any contact with the unconscious which is the ego's maternal matrix. Psychosis is just living in the perpetual grip of unconscious forces and abdicating the role of the ego altogether. The old adage says it well: The neurotic builds castles in the air while the psychotic lives in them. Jung saw this split in us, this living in only one dimension, as a religious problem and advises us that "all opposites are of God—therefore man must bend to his burden, and in so doing he finds that God in his opposite-ness has taken possession of him, incarnated himself in him. He becomes a vessel filled with divine conflict."[14]

I am therefore led by the story to the place of opposites within me. Gradually I am coming to discover over the years that there is a feminine side to my life as well as a masculine, that there is an anima as well as an animus. I recognize not only the virgin bride within but the shadow harlot. It is relatively easy to trot out the names of the opposites. It is easy even to admit intellectually to being the rapist, thief, drug dealer, murderer, etc. It is another thing altogether to experience them within and to acknowledge them, to claim them and accept them and yet until that is accomplished they have not really been encountered. The great poets like Dante in his journey through hell or the great mystics like Anthony of the Desert depict the meeting on the other side, and it is evident that it is a great trial. Perhaps many of us will not be expected to meet our shadows with such completeness, but without it we will not have become whole. It is in coming home to the opposites that we come to realize that life is not either/or but both/and. As I discover the opposites and accept them I discover also a new temple within me, for I come to understand that I can embrace all of life and not absolutize myself in only one part. I can accept the active and the passive, the dependent and the independent, the constructive and the destructive. If I cannot do this, then, as William Lynch has observed, "a life of repression and denial must become not an occasional need but the very definition of man. If I am or wish to be active I must crush the passive. Second, to grant place to one of the pair will be to take away all hope from the other essential wish and to make it despair. Finally it will strike at the very possibility of an innocent wish on the part of man. For whatever he does . . . will not be chosen as an innocent and separable absolute for its own sake."[15] The polarities must somehow therefore be brought into a unity which preserves their separateness even as it unites them.

In coming to the place of opposites within me I come home to the realization of the task that lies ahead, and now I see that too as comprised of opposites. From my side it involves "prayer, observance, discipline, thought and action,"[16] while I await from the deeper self the "hint half guessed, half understood"[17] that comes to lead me forward. In this place of opposites I discover that I have no need to go to a temple to pray, for I myself have become in my opposites a new temple of prayer where my "devotion to God's house burns in me like a fire" (v. 17).

Chapter 5
John 3:1—4:1
From Head to Heart

Nicodemus is one of those fascinating characters we meet in the gospel of John. He is the first in a series of people who come to Jesus for faith. He is followed rather quickly by a Samaritan woman and then by a pagan. In this way the circle of conversion is seen to widen from fellow Jews all the way to total outsiders. These people are important to John and to us because they provide a point of contact with Jesus which can lead our meditation. We will witness a good deal of diversity in the characters in the gospel and we will see how they provide alternate responses to Jesus as well as insights into our own existence. Jesus of course is at the center of all these exchanges, and it is through them that we also begin to catch a vision of his presence and how he operates in us.

The task that confronts us then is to try to discover who the Nicodemus is in our lives. What does he look like? Where do I most often confront him in my own existence, what are the relative strengths and weaknesses that he puts me in contact with? What was it that brought him to Jesus? What got him going? What motivated him? What happened when he met him and where did he go after he left him? These kinds of questions form a general background to my approach as I begin the story that John places before us.

Nicodemus, the first of these characters, appears in actual fact on three occasions in the gospel, and through a study of these three appearances it is possible to catch something of the conversion that is effected within him. The three appearances seem to document a change, from an initial curiosity about Jesus in chapter 3, to a willingness to speak on his behalf in chapter 7, to a final willingness and desire to enter as friend into his burial in chapter 19.[1] In a sense it is a movement from the more impersonal reason to the personal. Initially he comes with at least the possibility that he was motivated by a search for truth. He speaks because he is moved by a desire for justice. He remains even at the moment of death because of his respect and sympathy for the person of Jesus himself. Culpepper is not so generous in estimating his presence in the gospel. He feels that even at the moment of death Nicodemus expresses his grief by bringing expensive spices but he himself finds no life in Jesus' death. He is therefore for Culpepper one "who believes but refuses to confess lest he be put out of the synagogue. He is not far from the kingdom but he does remain outside."[2]

When first we meet this man we are given three facts about his life—not a great deal to be sure but yet each of them is significant.

1. He is a Pharisee. This is important and helps us understand something about the man. The Pharisees were a very conservative class of people. They emphasized the

importance of ritual, of tithing, of the laws of cleanness, purity, etc. By culture and training, therefore, we know that he is part of the upper strata of society.

2. He is also a member of the Sanhedrin. This was an elite within an elite. There were seventy members in the Sanhedrin and their group was presided over by the high priest. One might compare them with the Supreme Court in America. They possessed great power and were enormously influential.

3. Jesus calls him a teacher of Israel, a term that recognizes him as an authority within the field of education and formation. He was schooled and educated in the scriptures and culture of his people. He holds a position somewhat akin to a professor of theology in the church today. He is in consequence credited by his peers with a certain expertise and presumed by his contemporaries to be a man of knowledge and education.

All of this leads me to think of Nicodemus as an "upstairs man," a term I have taken from the TV series "Upstairs-Downstairs." He is an upstairs man not only in terms of his position, power, prestige, and scholarship, but also in terms of his preferences. He is a man at home in the world of thought, of ideas, of debates. He is a man of questions, and indeed the value of his questions are that they lead him to Jesus. Richard Viladesau points out how the "horizon of our questioning being is revealed as unconditional or absolute."[3] It reaches out to the infinite. Nicodemus reaches out through his questions to the horizon of his being, and he does so through logic and the rational thinking process. Martin Heidegger[4] in his *Discourse on Thinking* has made us aware of two modalities of thought (a) the calculative method which he says is rationalistic, economical, pragmatic, specific reductionistic and attached to the finite; (b) the meditative method which he finds best described as intuitive, contemplative, generalized, mysterious and drawn to the absolute. Nicodemus, it appears to me, fits well into the first category. He is a rationalistic calculative thinker.

We are told that Nicodemus approaches Jesus at "night." On the one hand this is not unusual, since "night is recommended for the study of the Torah and rabbis are often found prolonging their discussions well into the night."[5] However night has also other dimensions. It is a time when it is easier to hide, to avoid being seen, especially if one is in the company of a shady or unacceptable person. To the Jewish society at large Jesus was both. Why then does Nicodemus come at night? We are left with a series of questions. Is he the prudent man who comes to study the Torah and who does not wish to scandalize the community, or is he a person who is afraid of what everyone else thinks and so waits until darkness covers his behavior? Is he coming to Jesus because this is what he needs to do to discover what he wishes to know, or is he motivated by some other outside source to which he is now reaching either consciously or unconsciously? Is he positive or negative?

The more we look at Nicodemus the more he catches our attention. He is the carrier of the tradition, the custodian of the past, the bearer of the memory of the community. Nevertheless something seems to have cracked. Kysar[6] suggests that he is a representative person who in John's eyes designates those who would sacrifice their ties with their heritage in order to embrace the Christian faith. He certainly comes to Jesus, and he comes willing and wanting to embrace or at least hear about the new. The meeting is a particularly important one. There is in this meeting what

Culpepper calls "the pathos of age meeting youth, established religion meeting the emergent pneumatic movement, tradition confronting freedom. There is here the stricture of the legalist meeting the freedom of the moralist."[7] The dark of night, the questions that he poses, the shape they take, the shock at the received and unexpected response, are all clues and pointers to Nicodemus' character, and yet he escapes encapsulation. He fears and yet desires intimacy. He prefers knowledge to wisdom or at least it appears that way. He has difficulty trusting his own experience, preferring the conventional wisdom of the group, yet he is willing to risk it in search of Jesus. He is strongly vested in logical and deductive reasoning, although it appears that he suspects reason alone is not the answer to his quest. He is a man of power and knowledge, yet these have only brought him to a place in which he is both feared and frightened. He is a man of authority and status but comes under cover of night. Jesus' answer to him leaves us wondering if he is only a spectator and observer of his tradition or if he has gone on the long road that leads him to being an existential participant and visionary according to the images of his tradition?[8] Through the images Jesus seems to suggest that he has not learned the need to be born again, that he has not discovered what it means to be lost or saved, dead or alive. He is in the end quite an ambivalent figure. His is a theology of the mind and not of the heart. John Dunne points out the difference between the two when he says that "to see God with our mind would be to know God, to understand God; but to see God with our heart would be to have a sense of being known by God, of being understood by God."[9]

When we examine the dialogue between Jesus and Nicodemus we see that it really is a dialogue gradually becoming a monologue. Initially Nicodemus is in the forefront but gradually he fades away and Jesus' role becomes central. Jesus' comments become longer, larger, and more effusive as the dialogue progresses, while Nicodemus' answers get shorter and shorter until he is eventually silent. Jesus increases therefore while Nicodemus decreases, and this is an indication of the way things are in reality for John. We shall meet this pattern again in the gospel, notably in the dialogue with the Samaritan woman.

A second point worth noting in the dialogue is the questions of Nicodemus. Nicodemus' questions themselves reflect a progression as he moves from asking about the "fact" of birth, to asking about the "how" of birth, to asking about the "when" of birth. Jesus answers all three questions, although his answers are more reassurances than anything else. Perhaps he senses something of Nicodemus' frustration and moves to meet it. To the first question he says that birth is possible, but then he adds the postscript— not through your powers. To the second question he says that birth will happen through water and the Spirit. Finally, concerning the "when," he says that it will happen when the Son ascends to the Father. For John Jesus is the one who descends from on high. He comes to lead the people home, to give them Spirit life as opposed to flesh life. Jesus' task then is manifestation, to make the invisible visible, to show forth the presence of God and make him desirable, credible and lovable.[10]

It seems to me that this is not just a question and answer period between Jesus and Nicodemus in a philosophical or theological sense. I see it more as Jesus' offering a corrective to the one-sided development of Nicodemus. This is a role Jesus seems to play constantly in the gospel. When he meets the Samaritan woman, who in the midst of many relationships has no real intimacy, he provides intimacy for her by his care, concern and presence. When he meets the lonely man in chapter 5 he becomes for him the friend who enables him to discover community. When the crowds of chapter 6 are hungry he becomes their source of food, and when the blind man of chapter 9 cannot see, Jesus opens his eyes through his (Jesus') own vision. Even the dead Lazarus finds life when Jesus enters the wake scene and calls him forth from the tomb.

How does Jesus provide this compensatory view for the overdeveloped "upstairs" type of existence that we have been describing in Nicodemus? Karen Horney provides an interesting observation in a different context when she remarks that "the more the emotions are checked the more likely it is that the emphasis will be placed on intelligence. The expectation then will be that everything can be solved by the power of reasoning as if mere knowledge of one's problems would be sufficient to cure them, or as if reasoning alone would cure all the troubles of the world."[11] Nicodemus as we have been envisaging him is such a person. Nicodemus is in search of knowledge, in search of "gnosis" perhaps more than soul. He is seeking a knowledge that is quantifiable, that is accessible to reason—the kind of knowledge that resides in moral theology and philosophy, etc. Knowledge, however, as Jung says, "does not enrich us, it removes us more and more from the mythic world in which we were once at home by right of birth."[12] Jesus therefore breaks through this quest of Nicodemus' and offers a new kind of knowledge more associated with Sophia. It is a knowledge that belongs more to the moment, to the now, to the immediate. It is a kind of knowledge of the unknowable.

To achieve this Jesus first greets Nicodemus and gives him space. He gives him welcome and hospitality. Then he leads him back into touch with his own inner world. He reduces him from his inflated existence, his false sense of glory. He strips him of his apparent strength and renders him both answerless and questionless. He shows Nicodemus that his strength as a teacher of Israel is really a weakness since he does not understand and is unable to enter the metaphors of water and spirit. It seems to me that at this point Jesus is not unlike a Zen master asking his student: "What is the sound of one hand clapping?" Any attempt to answer the question by logical means is doomed to failure. One needs to come to a new place, a different perspective, in order to be able to respond. Jesus, it seems to me, is attacking the cause-effect type of thinking that has been normative for Nicodemus. He tells him that he must be born again, and Nicodemus is unable to comprehend what Jesus is speaking about. He is like the person Eliot describes in his famous question: "Where is the wisdom we have lost in knowledge?"

When Jesus tells Nicodemus that he must be born of water and spirit, he is inviting Nicodemus to a new life. Much has been made of this response as an allusion to the need for baptism, but as Schnackenberg points out, "Baptism in water is not the real focus of interest but birth from the Spirit. . . . His words are not connected directly with baptism but with the new creation by the spirit of God."[13] It is true that John is here using a core symbol of the gospel. Water has increasing importance throughout the gospel, and John uses it in different ways as the following chart indicates:

In chapter 1	It is the background for a discussion on baptism.
In chapter 2	It is in foreground as it is transformed into wine.

In chapter 3	It is essential for birth.
In chapter 4	It is an underground spring bubbling to life.
In chapter 5	It is a reservoir for healing and restoration.
In chapter 6	It is the mystery that frightens and attracts.
In chapter 7	It is a thirst within people.
In chapters 8–9	It is a way to sight.
In chapter 12	It is a symbol of service and a new way to live.

In using the symbol of water then at this junction, John is placing before us a very rich and powerful symbol. Jesus is obviously talking to Nicodemus of different spheres of existence. What is flesh is flesh, what is spirit is spirit, and he notes that people cannot of their own volition enter the sphere of spirit. There is an essential giftedness to this dimension of existence. One is invited to it. It is death to the conscious viewpoint. Nicodemus must enter the water; he must make a conscious decision to enter the path to the new. This is very difficult for him. Nicodemus is not a bad man—in fact, quite the contrary. He has achieved much to be proud of in his lifetime, and that is what makes the task before him now so difficult. He has worked hard to get this far. To be invited to the waters and to the Spirit now in a sense contradicts all the efforts of his life to this point. But it is the waters that give the Spirit, the essential giftedness of life, and Nicodemus must enter into these waters, into the unconscious which signals the new birth and affirms the reality of the Spirit or transcendent life. Nicodemus knows that this is death, the kind of journey and death that D. H. Lawrence speaks of in "The Ship of Death" when he says:

O lovely last, last lapse of death, into pure oblivion
  at the end of the longest journey
Peace complete peace
But can it be also that it is procreation?
O build your ship of death
O build it
O nothing matters but the longest journey.[14]

Nicodemus is here, it seems to me, invited to oblivion, to peace, to procreation, to the ship of death, to the longest journey, to the journey to the heart, to the Spirit.

I come now to this story of the meeting between Jesus and Nicodemus, and I come to it in prayer. In reading the story I find my primary identification is with Nicodemus. I can relate to him easily. I know what the years of study are like. I can relate to him in the search for knowledge, in the many books which surround me that represent the community of thinkers with whom I am in dialogue at the moment and also with whom I have conversed over the years. I come to this moment with many scripts for living which I have learned from them; some of these are conscious, some are still unconscious. In the presence of these thinkers I find a certain kind of comfort. There is the collective wisdom of the ages here before me, and at least in part I have ingested it, and to that extent it is quantified and codified for me. It enables me to make a "healthy" adjustment to the moment, and the scriptures and sacred texts passed down from one generation to another give me a sense of comfort and peace. I feel that I have worked hard, studied well, and been diligent in pursuing knowledge over the years. There is in consequence a sense of satisfaction within me, a sense of accomplishment, a sense of pride. As I reflect further on this I become aware of my own fondness and propensity to deal with all of life and all of reality, with everyone and everything from the head, from the past and from the known.

What then does it mean to meet Jesus? What that would look like is the question that the story invites me to look at and the journey it asks me to undertake. It would mean coming home to the depths within me, coming home to water and to Spirit. It would mean risking the unexpectedness of the moment. Recently this came to me in a very simple way. I was listening to a piece of music by Beethoven in the company of a friend of mine. On the way home following the performance we began to talk of the evening and how we enjoyed the music. When I was asked what I thought of it I found myself answering with observations like the following: I was wondering what Beethoven was thinking when he was writing this, how he envisaged the world, how the notes and sounds, the ups and downs, were clues to his vision, etc. My friend's response was that she felt filled by the music, uplifted and expanded. I was coming to the music from my head; she was coming to it from somewhere else—her heart if you wish. I have a suspicion that the music was Jesus inviting me to the waters, to the experience of each moment as a birth, and that in each moment I am coming to be. To hear Jesus at this moment means therefore to give myself over to what Bowden Howes calls the "Great Emergence" to cultivating an attitude "of affirmation, of facing that which is inside and that which is in the situation engaging with that which one encounters from inside and outside, engaging with it decisively and courageously."[15] It would mean risking what has been for the sake of what is.

To listen now to the story of Nicodemus and Jesus is to touch something within me, a nighttime that can be either positive or negative, an uneasiness that arises from the deep-seated suspicion that my own efforts and accomplishments, essential as they are and important as they have been, are not enough. There is a depth somewhere in me that invites me to be born again, to come to life again in this moment that is now, to come home to a life that is based not only on what is true but on what is good, that is, on value.

Chapter 6
John 4:1—4:41
From Forgetfulness to Memory

John follows the story of Nicodemus with a story about a woman from Samaria and her meeting with Jesus. The two candidates for the faith, as Van Den Bussche calls them,[1] are different in many ways. He has a proper name; she is presented under a rather anonymous title. He is a man; she is a woman. He is a male teacher of Israel; she is a "mere" woman of Samaria. He has position and power; she has neither status nor might. He has what to many could be considered "breeding" or lineage or noble birth; she has what is called a shameful and hidden past. He is a "pure blood"; she is a commoner. He has seen signs and knows that Jesus is from God; she not only has not seen signs but doesn't even know where he comes from. If Nicodemus' journey can be described as a journey from the head to the heart, from upstairs to downstairs, we can consider her journey as a journey from forgetfulness to memory.

The Samaritan woman, however, is not without her strengths just because she is initially presented as different from Nicodemus. She is a woman who is aware of her own tradition and in touch with the Jewish tradition. She knows and probably has suffered from the enmity that exists between the two groups. She is aware of the laws and institutions, the received attitudes and mores that regulate their meeting. She is honest and capable of responding openly to the questions that are addressed to her. She sees some of the shortcomings of her own cultural experiences even as she perceives the virtues that it has permitted her to evolve in her own life. She is a risk taker and is willing to trust the dialogue with him and to open herself in the most intimate of relationships with him.

Their meeting is more then fortuitous, as is evidenced by the many obstacles they both had to agree to overcome if anything was to happen at all. Among the obstacles that come to mind was the fact that Jews and Samaritans did not get along. There was a history to the hostility between the two groups that dated back to the fall of the northern kingdom in 722 B.C. The Samaritans refused to worship at Jerusalem. Furthermore they sided with the Syrians in their wars with the Jews and they put as many obstacles in the way of the Jews restoring Jerusalem as was possible.⁴ They were like the Irish and English today. Both their respective histories and cultures made it difficult for them to get along.

In addition to this there is a further obstacle in that he is a man and she is a woman. One of the rabbinical laws clearly stated that a man was not to talk to a woman in the street, not even to his own wife. This meeting takes place out in the open, and so it is quite public. A third factor mitigating against their meeting is the fact that it is noon. He, we are told, is tired and exhausted from the journey, and he has sent the disciples for food while he rests. This would indicate that he was also hungry and not in good shape for a lengthy conversation. She on the other hand comes for water at the hottest part of the day when it must have been toughest to get, and draw, and carry home the bucket of water. She is obviously avoiding doing so either in the early morning or late evening when it would be less strenuous. Her willingness to draw water at that hour of the day is an indication of her desire to avoid the crowds, the meeting with people, the conversations that occur on such occasions, etc. This meeting then is portrayed by John as a meeting of the outsider and insider, the feminine and masculine, the Samaritan and Jew, the inferior and superior.

The following chart represents the dialogue that takes place between the woman and Jesus. I have kept to a rather loose translation so that the general structure of the dialogue might be more easily observed:

JESUS	WOMAN
4:7 Give me a drink.	4:9 You are a Jew. How can you ask me for a drink?
4:10 If only you recognized God's gift and who it is asking you.	4:11 You don't have a bucket and the well is deep. How are you going to get flowing water. You are not greater than Jacob.
4:13–14 Everyone who drinks this water will be thirsty again. Whoever drinks the water I shall give will never be thirsty.	4:15 Give me this water so I don't have to keep coming here.
4:16 Go call your husband and come back here.	4:17 I have no husband.

4:18 Right you are in claiming to have no husband. You have had five.

4:19 I can see you are a prophet.

4:21–25 An hour is coming . . . when real worshipers will worship the Father in spirit and truth.

4:25 I know there is a Messiah coming and whenever he comes he will announce all things to us.

4:26 I who speak to you, I am he.

4:29 Come and see someone who told me everything.

It can be noted immediately that there are seven sections to the dialogue. In the beginning the conversation centers around the impersonal, but gradually it moves into the more personal sphere. They talk about water, then they begin to focus more on each other. They also talk in different time zones. Initially they are talking in a kind of conventional time zone. Then they moved to discuss the past, and then the future where they talk about the coming Messiah. Finally they enter the real present and address themselves to the current state of affairs.

The seven interchanges reflect a deepening intimacy between them. As he speaks there is a gradual unveiling of who he is. As she speaks there is a gradual acceptance of who she is. This acceptance of who she is corresponds to an expansion of vision, and the interesting fact is that as she accepts herself more she comes to see him more and more in his own uniqueness. He takes her, within the dialogue, from the land of forgetfulness to the land of memory where she can let go of denials and illusions and come home to the reality of her life. She need no longer defend herself, and so, as the story unfolds, she moves from seeing him ethnically as Jew, to seeing him stereotypically as prophet, to seeing him archetypically as Messiah, to seeing him in his totality as revealer who "told me everything I ever did."

The movement between Jesus and the woman can also be seen in another way. Initially, even though he is at the well when she arrives there, it is clear from the way the story is told that she is in charge. She has, it appears, access to all the resources—the well, the water, the bucket, the community, etc. She is running the show; she is in control, at least externally. His presence then is an intrusion. Even though he is already at the well, it is he who intrudes on her space, he who initiates the dialogue and he who issues the personal challenges in the story. She is rather defensive and protective of her personal privacy. She attempts to put distance between them; gradually, however, the barriers are lowered. Ian Ramsey puts it like this: "Thirsty Jew becomes strange water, purveyor, prophet, Messiah, and finally I . . . speaking to you."[3] She has tried to divert the conversation into the objectively neutral, the intellectually distant and the temporally confusing, but only the truth works to set her free.

What, then, we may ask, is really going on in the dialogue? It seems to me that what is happening is a movement between forgetfulness and memory. Thomas Kane[4] points out how easy and prone we are to live in "a forgetfulness of our own history, hiding from our painful past, out of touch with our elusive past," and how because of that we "live in a fog," not remembering or understanding where we came from, not seeing where we are now, drifting vaguely into the future. In this situation he suggests that a prayerful remembering can be vitally important. Such a remembering is important for this woman, and Jesus leads her to it with respect, caution, and clarity. In the process of remembering and forgetting, says Russell Holmes, a "relationship is established with the collective unconscious and the archetypes which carry a healing as well as a wounding function. . . . The center is arrived at by the function of forgetting and memory, and contact with it is maintained by remaining fluid in the sense of being able to recall the original energy of life and being able to forget the personal in favor of what transcends it."[5] Jesus, it seems to me, is helping the woman to this point. He activates her memory in the dialogue, leading her out of forgetfulness of her elusive and painful past. He remembers with her so that by calling her from forgetfulness he can trigger in her the much deeper memory of who she is before God. He enables her to tie into something larger than either the forgetfulness of her personal past or the painful memory of her personal life. That is why the conversation can end focused on the future.

The result of the dialogue, the meeting, the forgetting and remembering, becomes clear as the story draws to a close. She is led away from compulsive behavior which after all is behavior in bondage to the past. She no longer needs to repeat in a driven and unconscious way the pattern of the past. The scapegoats are confronted and eliminated. She is drawn beyond blaming the past, the other, the husband, the lover, etc. She is presented with a choice, and from the story it is clear that the choice is open-ended. The energy previously locked up in her defenses now becomes available to her for witnessing. She no longer needs to carry with her a lot of other stuff like water jars, etc. She is free to leave them aside and celebrate her conscience. She need no longer move only in the heat of the day to avoid people. In fact she can go to meet them. She becomes conscientious, jubilant and evangelistic, a woman proclaiming freedom and truth, given to mission and the benefit of the whole community. In moving through forgetfulness and memory she discovers there the rest of the universe.

The story of the woman at the well becomes my own story in prayer. She, like Jesus, corresponds to something in me. Van Kaam remarks that this story "is the tale of our excuses for not being compassionate with those who differ with us in background, ethnic, ethical, or religious persuasion. . . . Her resistance uncovers the core of the demonic system of resistance in each of us against being generous and gentle."[6] Here Van Kaam perceives her as being a pattern of activity and behavior that is resisting involvement and connectedness with all of life. This is helpful, but I recognize her in other areas as well. She is the presence in me of a whole group of needs and emotional upheavals that erupt from time to time and hold sway in my life. She clothes my anxieties and depressions, my loves and hates in all their passion. Her face is the face of all the inferiorities and incompetencies that I have kept away from consciousness for years. I look at her now and something is activated in me. I meet my forgetfulness in her as in a mirror. I look at her and it floods over me, and as that happens I am called out to name the unconsciousness that drives and claims my life. She is the memory of my forgetfulness as surely as the forgetfulness she reminds me of is but the mask of the deeper memory that he is.

My sense of the story then, as it is active in me, looks something like this: I begin to pray the gospel and my attention is attracted to the Samaritan woman. As I look at her I am gradually drawn by her face to an anonymous part of myself. As I watch her tell her life story and let it pour out, I become more and more aware that I too am driven. I begin to touch something of the compulsive searching and activity in my life. I become aware of how the search for intimacy in my life gets diverted into food or drink or some other pleasurable kind of experience. They knit my life together and shape something of the pattern of my existence, and they also are responsible for the moods of my life. When pleasure is high I feel good; I feel valued and valuable. When pleasure is low I feel misunderstood or abandoned or lost. It is not that this goes on all the time, but now in watching the woman at the well I become aware that it is part of my life. I have been living it unconsciously. It is a lived experience, but one that had not really been brought into my awareness and reflection. This is to say that it is an experience being lived in forgetfulness. The woman at the well mirrors that to me. She reminds me of my forgetfulness. She brings me home to an habitual anonymous dimension of my life.

But then I continue to read the story, and as I do my eyes now are more and more drawn to Jesus as he is present in the story and to the dialogue between him and the woman. Initially as I looked at the story I became aware of my forgetfulness where it seemed I was in control and had access to all the resources. However, now as I keep meditating on the Jesus-woman dialogue I become awakened to a desire, or a calling, or a thrust to want to live my life in response to something other than just pleasure. I want my life to be a response to meaning and to value. I want to be able to say that I had more than a good time while I lived. I want to know that my life made a difference, and somehow without even knowing the details I am grasped by a sense that this means I am responding to values, to the gospel values that I see in Jesus as he talks and encounters the woman. The memory of my forgetfulness, then, that I encountered in meeting the woman, leads me to a deeper memory wherein I begin to see what I did not see before, and this opens for me the call to and the possibility of transformation.

   It may be well to round off this chapter now by returning to the story and the symbol that runs through it which
for me is water. It is through the dialogue about the object
water that John is enabled to move the story. When he uses
water, however, he is using one of the core symbols of the
gospel. There are, says Culpepper, "conversations about
water, water pots, rivers, wells and springs, sea pools and
basins, thirst and drink in the gospel."[7] Here the water that
Jesus and the woman speak of is initially an external reality,
an object outside both of them, available to them at the well
of Jacob. In the story, however, it too undergoes a kind of
change so that the water they end up talking about contrasts sharply with the kind of water one gets from a cistern.
The water Jesus speaks of to her is best called "living"
water. That is a unique quality. It is not stagnant water,
fresh water, purifying water, washing water, etc. It is living
water. It is water that is active and dynamic. It becomes a
fountain, springing up, bubbling over, surging and cascad-
ing, water that is overflowing and constantly renewing
itself. Jesus makes it clear that this water is a gift, and that
it is given to her, and to me, in the dynamic movement from
forgetfulness to memory.

Chapter 7
John 5:1—6:1
From Isolation to Imagination

Loneliness is one of our common experiences. It seems to be something that enters everyone's life at one time or another. For some it is a transitory thing, a pause in what they might consider an otherwise connected life. For others it is the ambiance within which they have moved over a lifetime. It is in either case a very difficult experience for many people producing what Henri Nouwen calls either a "suffocating isolation" or a "creative solitude."[1]

Loneliness certainly produces its questions, whether they be "Why me?" or "What's happening to me?" or "Will it ever end?" etc. It invites the powers of the beyond, either evil or good, and so it becomes an important moment in life. What then shall I do with my loneliness, or what shall my loneliness do with me? What shall I do with the emptiness and the void that crowds in upon me in these moments? Shall I join the devils of self-destruction or the angels of winged inflation? How shall I cope with the rage that the apparent indifference around me generates within

me in the loneliness? What does loneliness say of me to me?
Or, to ask John Dunne's question, "What does loneliness
show of the heart's desire? What do we find if we follow
the heart's desire? Ourselves or something greater than ourselves?"[2] The questions multiply within me in the loneliness until the waiting for answers collapses and I discover
with Eliot that:

> I must be still, and still moving into another intensity
> for a further union, a deeper communion through the
> dark cold and empty desolation.[3]

John was no stranger to loneliness or to the questions
it evokes. In chapter 5 he brings together four elements that
are linked which may help us approach it. These elements
I call: (1) the sabbath; (2) the paralytic; (3) the Jews; (4)
Jesus. We will look at each in turn.

The Sabbath. We will approach this first since it is the thing
that connects the others together. It was on the sabbath that
the healing of the paralytic was effected, it is because it was
effected on the sabbath that the Jews reacted so strongly to
it, and it was because it was on the sabbath that he effected
the healing that Jesus was then able to develop his teaching
further in the discourse that follows. The sabbath therefore
is the Gestalt here; it is the background that illuminates the
foreground and allows us a deeper understanding.

We get a clear understanding of the importance of the
sabbath in the synoptic tradition. The charge brought
against Jesus there is based on the fact that he violated the
sabbath as a regular practice. John condenses that practice
into this single event. "Why does he do that?"we ask, and
a quick look at the next couple of chapters gives us a possible hint at an answer. It is part of a plan. In the trajectory

of the next five chapters we see him replace all the great Jewish feasts. Chapter 5 has the sabbath as background, chapter 6 has the Passover, chapters 7 through 9 take place within the feast of Tabernacles, while chapter 10 has as its context the feast of Hanukkah. Schillebeeckx observes that "on these feast days Jesus presents his unique and overwhelming particularity over against the theme of salvation brought through these festivals."[4] We begin by taking a larger look at the sabbath in Israel's history.

The sabbath was a weekly feast whereas the other feasts were celebrated annually. Etymologically the name appears to have come from the Hebrew verb "shabath" meaning to cease or to stop.[5] Different motives were given for observing the sabbath, but the one most generally accepted is that which stresses its religious character. This explanation derives from the priestly tradition. In this perspective the sabbath is seen as the sabbath of the Lord, a day consecrated to him. It is seen as a sign of the covenant, and to observe it was to be guaranteed salvation. Failure to observe it meant that one ceased to belong to, and be part of, the community. If the whole community failed to observe it, then it was understood that the people would incur God's punishment and wrath.

Initially the day was celebrated as a day of rest. All heavy work ceased and the people celebrated joyfully. When the temple was destroyed, things changed. The other major feasts were no longer celebrated, and so the sabbath assumed a new importance. Special rules governing its celebration were gradually introduced, and as time went by they became more solidified and rigid. Nehemiah closed the gates of Jerusalem to prevent the people from violating the sabbath, and later in history we see people in the time of the Maccabees allowing themselves to be slaughtered rather than violate this day. In the time of Jesus, then, it

comes as little surprise to find the Pharisees interpreting the
law regarding the sabbath in a very strict manner. In fact
they were adding even more rigid regulations. No work
whatever was permitted, with one exception I will mention
later since it has relevance to our scripture passage. It is this
day of the sabbath and these strict regulations that Jesus is
now accused of violating. The accusation therefore is that
in effect he has violated and profaned the covenant by healing the paralytic on the sabbath. Jesus as we shall see in a
moment responds to these accusations. This is the background that lights up the foreground of Jesus' action. This
celebration with its regulation regarding work, its percep-
tion of what is holy, its methodology of celebration, and its
insistence on the religious significance of action and inaction are essential to the story that follows.

The Paralytic. It is against this background that John now
presents us with the paralyzed man. He presents him to us
in a classical description of the lonely person. The description is remarkable because it is not only the external situation of the person that is presented but also his internal
disposition.

The man is certainly isolated. He is cut off from what
we might consider any of the normal and everyday sources
of support, comfort and encouragement. He has no family
and no friends. There are no doctors or nurses. There is
nobody who is available to him and nobody who is present
to him, and that is only the beginning. There is a second
factor hidden in between the lines. Everybody else, it
appears, has somebody, for the others are able to get to the
pool. Their availability can only heighten his own sense of
isolation. Furthermore he is in the place of the sick. All
around him are the blind and the crippled. This can sometimes be a comfort to the sick, but in his case it is a torture,
for he cannot get to the pool. One could say even more. He

is also hurt in his religious dimension of life, since he apparently doesn't even know that it is the sabbath. His ties to that event seem fractured at best and destroyed at worst. Its symbolism seems to be no longer working positively in his existence connecting him with the God of the covenant.

This man's situation is not new; it is not something that just happened. He has been like this a long time—in fact, thirty-eight years. Some see in this a reference to the length of time the Israelites wandered in the desert during their formative period as a people. Whether this is true or not is open to further debate, but it underscores the length of time this person has been incapacitated. In these years he has apparently become dejected, deflated and disillusioned. Raymond Brown says that "this crotchety grumbling about the whippersnappers that outrace him to the waters betrays a chronic inability to seize the opportunity, a trait reflected again in his oblique response to Jesus' offer of a cure."[6] Time has had a negative effect on him. He appears either unwilling or unable to assume responsibility for anything. He is content to allow Jesus to be the fall guy, to take the blame before the authorities. There appears to be a surfacing of rage, which indeed may explain why everyone left him. Loneliness can create a violence that not infrequently expresses itself in withdrawal and anger which often drives people away, thus intensifying the loneliness and creating a circle of despair.

This man seems dulled in his sensitivities. He has become accustomed to disconnectedness, not only from his family and friends, but, it appears, even from himself. He is not able to express his own needs, and he is no longer in touch with his own emotions, feelings and desires. When Jesus asks him if he wants to get well, he can only answer with a sense of despair. He exists in a no-win situation where everything must be endured even though he believes that nothing is possible. The overall tone then is that of an isolated disconnected person frustrated over his inability to reach the water (which of itself is an interesting symbol of life, unconscious, etc.) and who in consequence is feeling the burden and terror of despair and depression.

We must be careful, however, not to make the man into the willing instrument of his own torture and end up blaming him for being sick. It is suggested by the story that the man's situation is the result of a long period of predictable patterning. If his situation now is or appears hopeless, it is because he has not been able to get the help he needed from beyond himself. Hope, as Lynch points out, is not an "exclusively interior thing. . . . [It is not] an absolute and interior spark in man."[7] This person did hope perhaps at one point in time since he managed to get to the pool. Joan Chittister observes that the "paralytic didn't go to Bethsaida with faith; the paralytic knew the waters moved every year. The paralytic didn't go to Bethsaida with love; the paralytic knew God's gifts belonged to him. The paralytic went to Bethsaida in the hope of finding a teacher whose faith was performative, a teacher who would carry him down."[8] Now, however, it appears that the time has passed, for, as he says, "By the time I get there someone else has gone in ahead of me." In this situation the man is helpless. He is caught in his own closed web of thought and feeling. His perceptual sense has become contaminated. He is isolated and alone in what we might call, to borrow a phrase from Lynch, a "gnostic imagination" that sees the world as dangerous and destructive and in consequence of which everything has to be distrusted. He has at this point incorporated the "oppressive system into an actual living entity."[9]

The Jews. The Jewish authorities are the second group that we are presented with in this story. We have indeed already met them in the gospel but they have been relatively quiet.

From this point on they will assume a much more active and conspicuous part in the gospel. John will give them increasingly more attention and emphasis until they eventually become synonymous with darkness. The trajectory then from beginning to end is important. In the opening chapters Jewish leaders sent Pharisees to question John the Baptist. This procedure, this process of questioning, this interrogatory posture, remains one of their functions throughout the gospel, especially for the first ten chapters. They questioned John; then after the incident at the temple they question Jesus. This is followed by their presence in the person of Nicodemus who comes with his questions to Jesus at night. Here they question him about the sabbath and his authority to heal the paralytic on this day.

As the gospel progresses their questioning continues. John will show, however, that the questioning becomes increasingly more egocentric and self-serving. Their developmental trajectory then is increasingly manifested in a negative light. They receive here what Culpepper calls their "script for the rest of the gospel."[10] They will become more and more associated with all the negative categories and images in the gospel—categories like the world, sin, the devil, darkness, blindness and death. They are what Kysar calls "stylized types" which must not be confused with the Jewish people. John is not interested in them as people but as "foils over against his hero, the divine revealer."[11]

In chapter 5 they enter the controversy about the sabbath and the healing that has just taken place. It must be noted that they are not upset that Jesus healed the "man." In fact that does not seem to enter in any way into their deliberation. They do not seem to even notice that side of the event. It is the sabbath factor, for good or evil, that draws their attention. Jesus, they say, has violated the law, violated the sabbath, and therefore violated the covenant.

Did Jesus do this? Is he in fact guilty as accused? We noted above some exception to the general rule about the sabbath. One of these was that Jewish law would permit, in fact even require, Jesus to act on humanitarian grounds if the person was in danger of death. Since the man was in this condition for thirty-eight years, we could hardly say that this was the situation. Jesus' answer, however, makes it clear that he is not asking to be excused on humanitarian grounds. He claims rather to act on theological grounds, that is, that as God acted on the sabbath he was entitled to do the same. Their response to this assertion is immediate and instantaneous. They recognize that this means he claims to be God. They therefore now "seek to kill Jesus because he made himself equal to God" and this claim could not be tolerated.

In contrast with the paralyzed man's imagination we see here what we can call an "adolescent imagination." In this way of viewing things the world is not perceived as hostile. It is seen rather to be in error. This kind of imagination lives out of the past but does so totally unconsciously. It lives out a script that it is largely unaware of, and yet it lives it out intensely. It is characterized by the identification of all of reality with a little piece of reality, and the determined conviction that there is nothing else to be learned on the subject. The light of such imagination is indeed dim. It cannot allow for a light, a consciousness, a point of view other than its own. This imagination gets easily solidified. It becomes very quickly concretized into an institutionalized point of view with all of the advantages and disadvantages of that position. It is perhaps significant that the only relationship the Jews have with the paralyzed man, as later with the blind man in chapter 9, is that of interrogators. Their inquisitorial stance reflects an assumption that reveals their expectation. The paralytic, they assume, must answer their accusations and questions, and they believe that ultimately he must, and Jesus must, fit into their system of meaning, value and sense of ultimacy.

Jesus. Jesus is the third figure in the story, and he reflects a third kind of imagination. He is the one who heals the paralytic on the sabbath. He is the one who suffers the accusation, criticism, and questioning of the Jews. What may not be immediately apparent is that he not only heals the paralytic but he also offers to heal the Jews. He tries to draw them to a wider perspective. He does not deny their accusation but transcends it. He gives them grounds for either a greater and deeper accusation or a larger and broader vision. He claims the right to act on the sabbath. They choose the deeper accusation.

It should be noted, however, that while he claims to be God he does not consent to their accusation that he "makes himself equal to God." In 5:19–29 John is careful to point out that it is God who has made Jesus equal to himself, (1) in that he loves the Son and shows him all that he is doing himself, and (2) in that he has given all judgment to the Son. Here we must not understand judgment in terms that we normally associate with that word, that is, in a pejorative sense. Huckle observes that "Jesus is not a judge in that he labels actions which he observes as good or evil. He is judge in the sense that he creates the milieu and the occasion which provoke the person to behavior which will be either salvific or destructive."[12] (3) God has also granted Jesus to have life in himself. It is wrong therefore to say that Jesus is making himself equal to God. Rather it is, as Neyrey says, "God who loves, shows, gives, and grants Jesus certain powers so that all may honor the Son even as they honor the Father."[13]

What has been said here is consistent with what we have seen so far in the gospel. In 3:13–15 we were told that

Jesus alone came down from heaven. His origin is elsewhere. Thus in chapter 4 we are given a further understanding of his identity. We are told that he speaks for the
Father and reveals him. Now we are told that the functions
of God are the functions of the Son and that to respond to
Jesus the Son is to respond to God the Father, that to accept
Jesus is to accept God, and that to reject Jesus is to reject
God. We are growing, therefore, through the story in our
awareness of Jesus and his relation to the Father which
dominates the gospel. In this regard Augustine Grady's
observation is precise, that "John's gospel is a gospel of
pure relation in which the Father and Son are the indis-
solubly real pair, the two bearers of the primal relation
which from God to man is termed mission and command,
from man to God looking and hearing, and between them
both is termed knowledge and love."[14] In fact what is most
remarkable about John's theology is his use of the name
"Father" for God. In the gospel he uses the term one
hundred and seven times (twelve times in his epistle). The
whole system of his thought centers in the experience of
God as Father.

In the person of Jesus there is portrayed a third kind of
imagination which I wish to call "integrative" because it
incorporates all the other realities of the gospel story. (1) He
is enabled to accept the sick person as sick without blaming
him for his illness. At the same time he becomes for him an
offer of the future without limiting his freedom. He points
the man in a different direction and enables him to imagine
what he could not see before. (2) He can also accept the
sabbath and see it for what it is, a gift for man, without
destroying either its purpose of rest, or worship. (3) He is
also able to accept the Jewish lack of vision and consequent
hostility without limiting them in that perspective. He in
fact sees more in them than they see and he offers them that

perspective on themselves and life. He points them toward the very thing that anchors them, and he restricts their forward motion by saying: "You are looking for praise from one another," and he invites them beyond that through the image of Moses who it seems functions here in an archetypal way. (4) He accepts the Father as the source and goal of his journey with whom he is bonded and apart from whom he does not act. He acts only in communion with him because, as he puts it, "I am not trying to do what I want but only what he who sent me wants."

What Christ wishes then is what the Father wishes. At the same time it seems evident that what Christ wishes is not the Father's approval or acceptance. He does not fear rejection by the Father. That is more the kind of stuff that I find in my own act of wishing in the loneliness. I wish for a companion, or a friend, or someone who will be there for me. I wish for a presence so that I can give myself to someone or receive from someone. Christ wishing what the Father wishes, however, seems to be apart from any of that kind of stuff. It is more the open acceptance to whatever the Father wills.

The imagination of Jesus at work in the story is integrative and relational. It is freeing precisely because of this fact. It sees connections. It sees the world as relational and connected, which is, as I have suggested, what the sick person can't do and the Jews won't do. The paralyzed person sees the world in terms of abandonment and the Jews in terms of impersonal legislation, and their images for living come from that viewpoint. Jesus in contrast sees life as interpersonal, dynamic and in terms of community and mutuality. Their imagination disconnects and fractures life. It has an impoverished and shriveled viewpoint. It leaves things out on a limb. He proclaims life, even in the midst of isolation, loneliness and eventually death. Life, he says, hangs together. It does knit, it does mesh. It is to the credit of the paralytic and the sadness of the Jews that when they were presented with his imaging in freedom, the one could stretch out, relinquishing his own gnostic imagination, while the others could not abandon their adolescent viewpoint.

I come now to this story in prayer and, as I am with all the other stories, so, too, now I feel drawn to ask a series of questions. What is the pool in my life? What are these waters which when disturbed become an extraordinary if normal source of healing? Are these waters outside or inside? Are they the waters of the unconscious? Who is the angel, the messenger that disturbs them? Why can't I reach them? What is preventing me from being healed? The more I ask the questions, the more helpless I begin to feel, the more lonely I begin to feel. I touch it in my meditation in the realization that I cannot get to the waters, in my awareness that between me and my healing there is a great distance. It is then that I notice how my imagination becomes infected and in my isolation I begin to resent everyone else in the story. Who are these others in my life? They are all those other broken members of humanity with their smells of sickness and poverty and pain and illness.

It is not, mind you, that I feel like this all the time, and it's not that this is even what I might call a normal constitutive of my existence, but rather the story helps me in these moments to recognize what is going on in me. It becomes a revelation for me of my need for someone, or something, in those moments when my imagination has become soured, contaminated, and would lead me into further withdrawal as a defensive measure. In these moments of loneliness I find myself at war, not wanting to admit my own dependency needs and by their presence being made ever more aware of their existence. The story opens me, however, to their presence, to their value, and to the need to confront them.

Continuing to pray and reflect upon the story brings me to a new set of questions. Who are the Pharisees in me? How are they operating? As I listen I begin to hear the argumentation going on within, the battle for control. I begin in the loneliness to hear the voices of accusation and condemnation. As I listen, however, I recognize that these voices are not really interested in me. They look and sound like my voice, but more and more I begin to hear them as voices demanding perfection in accord with some external standard, voices that have become hardened in me through time—one might even say "institutionalized." These glutinous voices eat me up and leave me further isolated, stranded, cut off, and as this happens I have the strange feeling of being the victim of my own victimization, accused and condemned from within for my imperfection by the even more imperfect voice of my own imperfection.

It is then that I notice the day, the hour, the time. I become aware that it is the sabbath, the time when *chronos* becomes *kairos*. I wonder what is the sabbath in my life. Is it a place? A space? A moment? A background? A context out of which I live? How, I wonder, does the sabbath function in me? I find myself going over the story again and again, playing with it in different ways, allowing it to play with me. Gradually I find that something is happening in me. Praying this story now for the past four or five weeks has brought me to a quiet space within me, a kind of center. I think that this is the sabbath, the place in me where God is active and passive, at rest and at work at the same time. Here in this sabbath space I find that gradually the clamoring of my imagination and the noise of the other devouring voices recede like tidewaters. Maybe they will come back again. It's unimportant. Here I feel that I can disengage

from them. I can release them and let them cry themselves
out. Here I begin to discover also that my loneliness is not
as alive. Maybe it has become something else, or maybe it
is just that something else has replaced it, or maybe it is just
not that important to see now. What I find instead is my
own aloneness, and this intensifies as I stay here in the center, and it's all right.

In the aloneness I begin to notice how my eyes are
drawn to Jesus in the story and to his questions. Do you
want to be healed? How different the voice in the aloneness
is to the voice in the loneliness. How different is the
empathic question to the accusatory one, how different the
two kinds of presence feel and yet how similar in some
ways they look. But I wonder whose voice is this in the center of my aloneness. Is it mine, Christ's or God's? What
mystery or who addresses me from these depths? This is the
final question of the story. It remains the unanswered question in my mind.

Chapter 8
John 6:1—7:1
From Object to Subject

There are very few of us who have not been misunderstood at one time or another in our lives. There are many different ways in which we have perhaps responded to that event. Sometimes it has evoked anger and we have gone on the defensive; sometimes it has led us to step back and ask ourselves whether that is what I really said; sometimes perhaps we have gone along with the misunderstanding as if that is what we really meant; and I'm sure also there are times when we have thought it important enough to go ahead and clarify the matter. We say: No, that's not what I meant, or What you heard is not what I said—this is what I said or meant, etc.

If such is our experience, it can be helpful in reading John's gospel, and particularly as we will see in this sixth chapter, because misunderstanding is one of the distinctive features of his gospel and of this chapter.[1] Sometimes this comes about in the gospel because Jesus will use double meaning statements, and just like a lot of our double mean-

75

ing talk, they will be used to seduce us into a second and less obvious level of meaning. The misunderstandings then are a way for Jesus to go on and give an explanation or discourse of the second or deeper meaning. We have had some examples of this already—e.g. in the cleansing of the temple the Jews understood him literally; in the Nicodemus story Nicodemus understood birth in a physical sense; in the story of the Samaritan woman "water" becomes a misunderstood phrase and later on Jesus will speak of himself as the living water, etc.

What we have in chapter 6 to begin with are two stories that are related to each other by a kind of misunderstanding. In the first story, which we have come to know as the "multiplication of the loaves," we are told how the crowds follow Jesus because they see the great work he is doing. Jesus notices their plight and how hungry they are and so invites Philip to consider how they might feed them. Philip doesn't know and thinks the task rather impossible. Andrew volunteers some information and help by bringing to Jesus a young boy and a few fish. Jesus blesses the bread and gives it to the crowd, and when they have finished eating twelve baskets are gathered. The crowd sees this and in their enthusiasm they want to make him king. This is what constitutes the misunderstanding. He is not that kind of king. Who Jesus is cannot be adequately expressed in this manner. There is something else that needs to be said, and that must be said about him.

To this end we have therefore a second story from John. It is presented as happening a little later in the evening when the disciples got back into the boat and headed for Capernaum. The story tells us that a strong wind came on the lake, and in the storm the disciples saw Jesus coming toward them walking on the water. He spoke to them and said, "Do not be afraid; it is I" (ego eimi). This is for John the corrective to the first misunderstanding.

The words "ego eimi" (it is I), which he uses in this second story, are used many times in the gospel by John. The difficulty is that they are not always used in the same way. Raymond Brown[2] distinguishes three general uses of the phrase: (1) when it is used in an absolute sense, e.g. "You will surely die of your sins unless you come to believe that I am" (8:24; cf. also 8:28; 8:58; 13:19); (2) when it is used with an explicit predicate, with a definite symbolic object, e.g. "I am the bread of life" (6:35); there are thirteen such occasions in John and I will refer to these below; (3) when it is used with an "implied predicate" as it is in the phrase in 6:20 that we are studying here.

Since there are different uses of the phrase, we must now ask the meaning of it here. Is it an assertion of identity in an everyday sense? Is Jesus saying to the disciples, "It is I," in a way somewhat similar to what we say when someone comes upon us unexpectedly? Or is this an epiphany Jesus? Is Jesus saying something here about a manifestation of God? Kysar holds to the second interpretation saying that the "I am" formulation signals the speaking of God. In the Old Testament the phrase is used to designate the speaking of God, and so Kysar says, "Out of both the Hellenistic and Jewish background John drew the idea of the use of this construction in connection with divine revelation."[3] As God spoke his own name, so now Christ may speak the divine name. Jesus is not just a breadman, or miracle worker or prophet. The special emphasis given to the phrase "ego eimi" forces a different interpretation and orients the story much more precisely. Jesus' greatness is that he can bear and claim the divine name. This is who he is, and failure to perceive that is failure to perceive him.

The story continues. Jesus had just fed the people. They followed him across the lake. John draws our attention to the Passover feast by reference to many little events (it was the time of Passover, the crossing of water, the feeding of the multitude, the presence of manna), and that is important for him, as we pointed out in the last chapter. The people ask Jesus now to give them "manna" as Moses gave their fathers manna in the desert a long time ago. Jesus tells them that it is his Father who gives them the real bread from heaven. They want his bread. They ask him for it, but it is apparent that again they are misunderstanding. Schnackenburg says that "the experience of feeding did not lead these people to a deeper vision. Their eating of the loaves gave them pleasure but it was enough for them to have their stomachs filled. Their thoughts and searching have no higher object."[4] Jesus responds to their desire to have a perpetual supply of such bread available by speaking to them of this bread, at a second level of meaning, in the great Eucharistic discourse.

He begins with the words, "I am the bread of life." I mentioned above how this is one of thirteen occasions where Jesus uses this phrase with an explicit predicate. These thirteen are generally reduced to seven different statements as follows:

1. I am the bread of life (6:35,41,48).
2. I am the light of the world (8:12; 9:5).
3. I am the door (10:7,9).
4. I am the good shepherd (10:11,14).
5. I am the resurrection and the life (11:25).
6. I am the way, the truth, and the life (14:6).
7. I am the true vine (15:5).

What is interesting about these statements, as Brown indicates, is that the stress is not always on the "I," for "Jesus wishes to give emphasis to the predicate which tells something of his role."[5] He sees therefore in these statements not a description of who Jesus is in himself but rather who he is in relation to man. The predicate indicates something important, therefore, to which we must attend. In the two misunderstandings we have an opportunity afforded to Jesus, to which he responds, to say who he is in himself and who he is in relation to people.

In the bread of life discourse, who he is in relation to people is now further explored. It seems to me that as the discourse develops John subtly adds to and changes the image so that an evolutionary understanding begins to emerge. If I just list them here, you can perhaps see what I mean. He calls himself in turn the "true bread," "the bread of God," "the bread of life," the "bread which gives life to the world," and finally the "living bread." In all of these he is giving his life for others. Arturo Paoli says that the ambiguity of the Eucharist is found in this: "My body and my blood, but for others, for something beyond, for something besides, for something deeper and I would say for something truer."[6] Jesus is giving himself as life, as nourishment to others. He is their connection between time and eternity, between each other, and within themselves. It is of course the latter aspect of this that we are exploring in our meditations. Jesus here is indeed for others. He goes, as Paoli suggests, to the "heart of the three great problems of man and these are the problems of the identity of the person with himself, communication with others, and freedom, which is the problem of becoming a person and growing in relationship with others and with things."[7]

The gift that Jesus gives his disciples, and all those who come to him, is in fact, if you believe his words, neither political leadership nor food but rather himself. The gift of self is what is at the heart of the Eucharistic discourse. The self is gift of self. What Jesus brought to people was not just bread or healing or recovery from illness, etc. It was life itself, and it was in giving himself to them that he called them to wholeness. The other side of Jesus' being for them is also portrayed in this discourse and that is who they become as he continues to give life and nourishment to them. It seems to me that as the story unfolds there is a change being asked, and that this growth and development in them is hinted in the following verses:

No one who comes to me shall ever be hungry (v. 35).

No one who comes to me will I ever reject (v. 37).

No one can come to me unless the Father draw him (v. 44).

Anyone who eats this bread shall live forever (v. 51).

If you do not eat the flesh of the Son of Man and drink his blood you will not have life in yourselves (v. 53).

He who feeds on my flesh and drinks my blood has life eternal (v. 54).

The man who feeds on my flesh and drinks my blood lives in me and I live in him (v. 56).

The man who feeds on me will live because of me (v. 57).

The development here as I see it is from fear and toward union. It begins with the central statement that unless a bond is effected there can be no life. The bond is guaranteed from the point of view of Christ. He will not reject, turn aside, or negate. The statement or discourse goes on then to say that this growth follows upon the discovery of graciousness, of being drawn and called. Then there is affirmation and fulfillment. Initially the discourse talks about a living "from" and "for" and then a "living because of." As it is further projected out in the gospel it grows even deeper and richer. It becomes an "abiding in" and a "remaining in" until in chapter 15 it finds a new expression in the metaphor of the vine and the branches. Here there is a give-and-take envisaged. It becomes a question of the vine living in the branches and the branches remaining in the vine. Michael De La Croix comments wonderfully on this metaphor as follows: "The vine exists first and it is from it that the branches spring, and it is also in it that they are united to one another. . . . However the vine is also in the branches through the sap which circulates through them and without which they will bear no fruit . . . and though the sap comes from the vine it is the branches that bear fruit and not the vine. There is then a growth through a reciprocity in love, and an abiding in each other, and the development of a new axis between them."[8]

But if there is a positive development there is also a negative development envisioned. Jesus offers himself to them as life, and as Crossan[9] points out there is in this sixth chapter a relationship between feeding and teaching, between bread and revelation, between Jesus the feeder and Jesus the food. The source of food becomes the revealer, the consumer becomes the believer, the temporary life becomes eternal. Jesus however in all of this insists that they accept this gift that he gives in the way, the manner, and the form in which he offers it. They cannot accept that, and so we see the negative road opened up. They are shocked, appalled and scandalized by the incarnational modality in which he offers himself. The hostility grows and expands as the revelation develops and becomes more stated. The murmuring becomes more pronounced. First they are questioning him in the chapter; then they look for signs; then an angry argument starts among Jews; then the disciples join forces and find it a "hard saying" and they do not want to listen to it anymore. Finally "many of his followers turned back and would not walk with him anymore." It is precisely his insistence that he is their food that triggers this response in them or, as Kysar puts it, when he calls Jesus' teaching here a scandal, "the offense that comes to expression here is really the offense of the Incarnation."[10]

The chapter therefore is a very powerful one with a number of themes. We have a statement of Jesus regarding his own identity together with a statement of who he is for us. There are indications of the need for a bond between Jesus and the disciples, with a consequent development, which can be either positive or negative, being outlined, and all of this takes place within the context of the Passover feast. It is indeed, as Kysar has suggested, a "drama that moves from the heights of enthusiasm to the depths of unbelief. And between are the scandalous claims which Jesus makes for himself."[11] God's presence in Jesus is perceived as challenging the meaning of their lives. He calls into question their values, their intentions and even their commitments. He invites them to a new and enlarged definition and understanding of who he is himself and who he is for them and in the process calls them to redefine themselves and the meaning of their own lives.

"What would this mean in terms of a story of self or what might it look like in a person's life?" was the question I found myself asking as I read the story. What are the different aspects of the story pointing toward and how are they part of me? What does the story ask of me or require of me? It was in the process of asking these kinds of questions and praying them that I gradually became aware that in some ways I was undergoing an experience of the story itself.

Initially as this suspicion began to dawn upon me I

found that my primary identification was with the people who ran around the lake after Jesus. They were in search of a kind of magical answer to the problems of existence. This magical answer was perceived to lie in receiving power, and I began to see that in a real way that was what I too was after. I became aware that the "I" that was active in reading, praying and searching out the story was the "I" of power. The more I stayed with the story, however, and let it play its way in me, and lead me, the more I began to "suspect," "intuit," "wonder" about something else. As yet I couldn't name the intuition, but it felt as though the "I" of the first moment in prayer was not the only "I" in the story. In and through the story I sensed another "I" coming at me or toward me, emerging from within or from without I am not sure, but its presence was unmistakable; it was in fact the presence of a question that was more than merely intellectual.

At this point, even though it was only the presence of an intuition/question, I found that now I was more in touch with the response of the disciples in the story. I began to hear part of me saying: "This couldn't be. This is a hard saying and who can hear it? This goes against all that I have been taught. This is blasphemy. This is unthinkable." In other words, as I found myself thinking about the relationship between the little "I" and the greater "I," between the "power complex" and the emerging intuition, between the unknown truth ahead in the moment and the guaranteed truth behind in the past, I found in me a sense of shock, of panic. Should I banish the thought or pursue it? Should I condemn the "unthinkable" for being "thinkable"? Should I move toward truth and life, or move away? Should I follow my desire to trust my intuition, or abandon it? At this point I began to see myself in the story as the disciples who found "him" altogether too much for them, who were joining the ranks of the murmurers and who found the "saying" a hard one and therefore could not hear it.

For a while I joined these disciples and let my question bury itself, but still I could not turn away from it altogether. I think this is true because in the question I believe that something of ultimate meaning approaches, that something of truth, something of life addresses me. Now the question translates itself for me as: "Is the self God?" My little "I," which I know is not God, asks a question of the larger I that I sense but do not know. I ask "Are you God?" and after the initial recoiling from the question described above I now live in the mystery of not knowing. At this point in my journey I feel more like the disciples who follow Jesus, saying, "You have the words of eternal life." The "self" that I am not draws me onward and must reveal itself. For Jung the "self" always remains beyond, calling and summoning people forward. One must negotiate the self rather than identify with it, for that would be to fall into inflation, and to come to hold some partial completion as total. This would then eclipse any further growth. And so as the story ends I find myself now hearing the "ego eimi" uttered, but I feel more like Peter when he was asked if he would go away. He answered by saying, "Lord, to whom would we go?" I feel like him. I remain in the not knowing even though I have heard the words. I remain in the question because I do not know what else to do, and to remain in the question is the only thing I can do, and in doing that I feel alive, I feel related, I feel summoned.

Chapter 9
John 7:1—8:58
From Discussion to Decision

I grew up as a city boy in a land of farmers. I cannot say that I know much about farming—just enough to tell which was the field and which was the road—but I did have the opportunity to hear them talking especially at nighttime when they came to my uncle's bar for a few drinks at the end of the day's work. They were a pleasant group of people for the most part. Generally they were not very talkative, or if they talked it was in a quiet tone. Perhaps farmers the world over are the same. It was inevitable that during the course of an evening someone or other would mention the weather. Then it was difficult to understand the farmer, especially if you were a "city boy" on summer vacation from school. It seems they were the toughest people in the world to keep happy. If it was wet they would mourn and weep about how they couldn't save the hay. If it was dry they would complain that the crops had no water. If it was cloudy something else wouldn't work. It is of course the same the world over in farming communities at the time of harvest. Perhaps that's why many of them have special feasts or celebrations or dances once the harvest is gathered.

The Jewish people were no different. They had a special feast each year at the end of September or beginning of October to celebrate, to sing, to dance and to give thanks for the harvest. It was known as the feast of Tabernacles or Booths,[1] and in many cases, since it was the most popular of all their celebrations, it was frequently just referred to as "the feast." As with the other feasts it was customary on this occasion for those who could to go to Jerusalem and to participate in the rituals that formed the celebration. Two of these rituals, as we shall see in a moment, were important to John, and he will use them to speak of Jesus.

Our story in chapters 7 and 8 begins with the brothers coming to Jesus and asking him to "go up" to Judea for the feast so that he could manifest himself to the world. What they had in mind was probably that Jesus at that time should show forth his power and glory. It would fit in well with the events because it was customary for the priests to meet those coming for the feast at the gate of the city and to form with them a joyful and happy procession. Of course, since many people came, it was natural also that people from different areas and nations would be boasting about themselves so that national feelings would run high on these occasions. The disciples saw this therefore as an opportune moment. There is, however, another meaning to the word "go up"[2] *(anabanein)* as the *Jerome Biblical Commentary* suggests. It evokes the idea of the resurrection *(anabasis)*. It is therefore perhaps this second meaning that John has in mind when he has Jesus say no to his brothers' invitation because "it is not time for me." Further indications of this meaning can be found in the fact that four days later he appears in Jerusalem during the middle of the feast. He had, it appears, made a decision to attend even if it was "as if in secret and not for all to see."

When he arrives in Jerusalem he goes immediately to the temple (7:14). Here he becomes involved in teaching in the synagogue. It is this teaching that John presents to us in chapters 7 and 8. It is presented as a series of dialogues in "reverse parallelism," as scripture scholars term it, between Jesus and the people. It is evident, however, that the Pharisees are very present to the situation and that they in fact send the temple guards to arrest him. In this series of dialogues we can see the following arrangement[3] which allows the fourth dialogue to assume the central position:

Dialogue	(1) 7:14–24 Jesus compares himself to Moses as a teacher.	(7) 8:31–59 Jesus compares himself to Abraham as a liberator.
Result	Why are you trying to kill me?	They want to kill me.
Dialogue	(2) 7:25–36 Jesus announces his departure and they will be unable to find him.	(6) 8:21–30 He is going to leave them and be lifted up on a cross.
Dialogue	(3) 7:37–44 Jesus offers himself to them as life, as water.	(5) 8:12–30 Jesus offers himself to them as light.

Dialogue (4) 7:45–52. This dialogue then emerges as the centerpiece. The others take their meaning from this, and so it is the dialogue that leads our meditation. The structure of the section itself becomes our guide. Even before Jesus got to Jerusalem we are told that "there was much whispering about him in the crowd. He is a good man, some people said. No, others said, he fools the people." Now, however, not only are the people arguing about and discussing him, giving their pros and cons, but the very authorities themselves are in turmoil and confusion. When the guards who are sent to arrest him return to the chief priests and are questioned relative to why they have not carried out their assigned task they reveal how impressed they are with him. "Nobody," they said, "has ever talked the way this man does" (7:46). Nicodemus reappears now and speaks on Jesus' behalf, saying that "according to our law" you can't condemn a man without a hearing. He argues against those who oppose Jesus, and so the very Sanhedrin itself is divided. The problem, as someone has said, was that Jesus showed up. He himself emerges as the "problematic." He is at once the call to faith and the stumbling block.

The fourth dialogue therefore reflects the problem and reveals the issue. Jesus is the problem and Jesus is the issue. The context is a liturgical feast and the call is for decision. People must choose. John, says Crossan, "is warning his Christian audience that it is in liturgical confrontation with their God that they make a commitment for or against the vision of love that has happened in Jesus of Nazareth."[4] The presence of Jesus, his very appearance, invites some to loyalty—they are stirred deeply and called to follow—but it moves others to murderous rage and jealousy. Either way however a decision is inevitable, and perhaps a brief consideration of the two symbols of water and light will help us further understand the necessity of this choice. These two symbols are the background to dialogues three and five, respectively:

1. It was customary for the people to pray during the feast for rain. In this way they sought assurance that life would continue, that the land would be fertile and fruitful. Raymond Brown says that "a procession would gather on each of the seven mornings of the festival. They would go down to the fountain of Gihon on the southeast side of the temple which supplied water to the pool of Siloam. There a priest filled a golden pitcher with water while the choir sang, 'With joy you will draw water from the wells of salvation,' which is part of a reading from the Book of Isaiah."[5]

2. During these ceremonies you also had the ritual lighting of the great golden lamps, the court of women was illumined and dances were performed with torches. Van Den Bussche tells us that this "pantomime was a commemoration of the time when Israel walked in the desert behind the pillar of fire which manifested the presence of God."[6]

Jesus takes over these two symbols, water and light, and applies them to himself, saying: "If anyone is thirsty, let him come to me. . . . Streams of living water shall flow from him" (7:38), and also: "I am the light of the world. Whoever follows me will have the light of life and will never walk in the darkness" (8:12). These symbols used for the law, which for the Jews was the ultimate revelation, are now taken over by Jesus. It is also interesting to note here that these symbols represent the opposites of feminine wisdom coming out of the water to nurture and sustain, and masculine wisdom coming from the light to distinguish and illuminate with clarity. Not only that, but a little later, in 8:21–30, he takes over the name of God himself and applies it to himself. "When you lift up the Son of Man, you will know that I Am who I Am." This name associated with the feast of Tabernacles and used in Judaism to express the hidden name of God is now taken over by Jesus. Decision about him therefore is inevitable.

What kinds of decisions then are made about Jesus? We tend to think that there are only two possibilities, either acceptance or rejection. However the gospel shows many different responses. Some of these we have seen already, but it is important to gather them together here in one place so that a trajectory between the two poles of acceptance and rejection may be perceived. Culpepper[7] lists what he believes are seven responses:

1. The first response of all is that of Judas. It is the response of defection. It is "infamous Paradigm." He leaves Jesus and the apostles and goes out into the darkness.
2. Rejection characterized primarily in the gospel by the Jews, who love the darkness rather than the light and the glory of men rather than the glory of God.
3. Acceptance of Jesus without open commitment as one finds in the "secret" disciples like Joseph of Arimathea, Nicodemus and possibly Pilate. They are compromised by their need for security and their positions guarantee them that much.
4. Acceptance of Jesus as a wonder worker. They come to Jesus and decide for him because of the "powerful" things he does. They are attracted to him only by their own egocentric projections. Here one thinks immediately of some of the people we mentioned at Cana, and of those who followed him round the lake at the multiplication of the loaves.

5. Acceptance of Jesus on the basis of his words. These people do not receive a sign but they listen to Jesus and are attracted by what he says. Good examples here are the Samaritan woman and to a certain extent the royal official's son.

6. Those who accept Jesus in spite of misunderstandings. These are in large part the disciples. Most of them misunderstand Jesus in one way or another. In this regard we think of Peter who cannot accept Jesus' death and Thomas who cannot accept his resurrection.

7. This is the group who accept Jesus, who give us the best example of what deciding for Jesus looks like. Culpepper calls this response "paradigmatic discipleship." It is evident (a) in those who overcome misunderstanding eventually, as we see in Peter's proclamation of love, Thomas' confession of faith, etc., and (b) in those who have no history of misunderstanding, like Lazarus, Mary, John the Baptist and John the Beloved Disciple who is, says Culpepper, the one who "abides in Jesus' love, believes, and bears a true witness. . . . He is the ideal disciple."

Thus while it appears that only two possible decisions exist, it is apparent that they are gradations along the trajectory from one to the other, and perhaps that is where many of us will find ourselves, not in either the ultimate positive or negative ideal, but in both this/and that.

I come now to this feast of Tabernacles and pray it as a story of self. It means coming to that place in me where I appreciate life, that place in me where I can and do express thankfulness for the harvest, that place where I pray for further growth, for the crop to continue into the future to assure me of life. It means coming home to myself as farmer in some way, to touch the earth roots of my existence. In this place I am confronted with a decision about the deeper

self. Is this deeper self, this Christ within, in reality the light
I can trust and the water that will slake my thirst? I find
myself becoming aware of the decisions that I have made
in my life, and not only the decisions themselves but the
"pattern" of decision making in my life. It is not then only
my commitments that are being focused here but the manner in and through which I make commitments. I find
myself paying attention to the way the temple guards made
theirs. They were attendant on, attentive to, and aware of
Jesus as someone unusual. I become aware of the Sanhedrin
decision based on assumptions about the way life has been
and therefore "must be." I am aware of Nicodemus deciding by not deciding, making decisions by postponement. I
look at each of the other groups I mentioned above and see
the pattern of their life and in them become confronted with
my own process.

Slowly as I watch the feast of Tabernacles unfold I
become aware of my own style of decision making. I begin
to acknowledge all the decisions in my life that were really
abdications. I see how many times I have backed into decisions, deciding by not deciding because I was not desirous
of really committing my life at all but rather desirous of
avoiding something else. I become aware of how often I
have masked any decisions by not revealing what I really
thought, felt, or wanted. I look to my choices and see how
many of them are penetrated with fear rather than freedom.
I see how I have so virtuously struggled to find the right
way, or the right solution, or the right answer because I
didn't want to trust and risk my way, my truth, and my
answer. I see the frequency with which I have made decisions by formula rather than by insight, decisions by lazi-
ness rather than by any deliberate process of work and
reflection.

But I also am aware of other moments and other kinds

of decisions that were based on knowing what I was doing in the moment, that were taken in response to my own truth. I do recognize that some of the decisions in my life were taken only after I had cast off the deceptions and illusions I was using to hide under, decisions that were taken when I had withdrawn from others the projections I was throwing onto them. These were decisions taken in the light following the looking into the darkness. To look to my choices then is helpful; to fail to do so is to "fail to see how the distresses of choice are our chance to be blessed."[8]

Chapter 10
John 8:1—8:12
From Bondage to Freedom

John tells us the story of the woman taken in adultery in chapter 8. It is a story that only appears in his gospel and one that became very important for the Christian community. It was not always that way. In fact the story did not get inserted into the gospel until much later on. Different reasons for this delayed entrance are given by exegetes.[1] One that seems to be fairly common is the hypothesis that such a story was an embarrassment to the early church. In the early church an adult was received into the community through baptism. At this time forgiveness of sins was seen to take place. Paul in his images captures this idea by talking of getting rid of the "old man" and putting on the "new man." The new life was seen to be totally different to the old way of life. It involved new values, a new spirit, a new way of thinking, and a new way of behaving. It was not considered possible that, once one turned away from the old life, he would ever turn back to it again. In fact this was so deeply ingrained into the life of the catechumens that many of them delayed baptism until later life lest the passion of youth lead them away from the new life with God. The story of Jesus and the woman in adultery was therefore difficult for the church to explain. He seemed all too ready to forgive her.

Now, however, the story, instead of being an embarrassment to the community, is one of comfort and compassion that manifests the face of a caring God who understands our failures and comes to lead us beyond them. The story as it is currently placed seems to interrupt the flow of chapters 7 and 8 as we have outlined them above. Crossan[2] for that reason suggests that it is probably best read as an appendix to those chapters. There are reasons, however, why the story has been inserted in this position by John. It does seem to fit in well with some of Jesus' statements in these chapters—e.g. he says that whereas the Pharisees judge according to the flesh he himself judges no one. The story illustrates that point. Here he also invites them to convict him of sin and they proclaim his innocence by their inability to do so.

The story itself is best understood as a "trap" story. We have seen numerous examples of these in Mark's gospel.[3] In these stories the attempt is made to place Jesus in the middle of a predicament so that no matter which way he acts he can be perceived to be in the wrong, and therefore open to condemnation. The two elements of the trap here are: (a) the Mosaic law; (b) the Roman law.

In accord with the Mosaic law, as it is given in Leviticus 20:10, both the man and the woman who were involved in this situation should be sentenced to death. How this was to be carried out was not stipulated in Leviticus, but Ezekiel describes the process in 16:38 as death, normally brought about by stoning. If Jesus excused the woman or let her go free, or failed to condemn her for the adultery, then he would violate the law. On the other hand, if he did condemn her to death, then the second part of the trap would be sprung because the Roman authorities had forbidden the Jews to impose the death penalty. Clearly therefore Jesus has been placed in an apparently "impossible situation." When one reads the story, one cannot help but be attracted to its simplicity, and yet its power is nearly overwhelming. It opens us to questions about our own sexuality and morality. It asks us to what extent we are willing to go in order to trap the innocent and guiltless one, what truly motivates us—care for the woman, concern for the law, desire to outwit the other, our own pleasure, etc.? The story is at once therefore simple and complex. It moves with great energy in a short space through its principal characters, the Jews, the woman and Jesus.

The Jews' standing in the story once again reinforces their negative position. They are here a foil for Jesus. The words that describe their actions reflect a certain cold-bloodedness. They "caught" the woman in the "very act" of adultery, which is not an easy thing to do in any society. It leaves one wondering if they were spying on her or if it was a set-up. This is especially true when we notice that her companion is not brought to Jesus (and the law would demand his death also). Why is this? Does it reflect a certain collusion, a double standard of morality, etc.? Then we are told that they "brought" her to Jesus which suggests a certain amount of coercion, and that they make her stand in the middle of the group "early in the morning." The true reflection of their intentions, however, is given in the line that tells us they were trying to "test Jesus," trying to trap him. They are revealed therefore ultimately as not being really interested in either the man who ran away, or the woman whom they have so easily exposed, or the law which they claim to be the object of their concern. None of these really moves them, only the desire to get Jesus. They are the true adulterers in the story. In fact they are worse. They are rapists motivated not by care for any person but by an underlying violence to get Jesus.

The woman's presence in the story is very strong, and yet she says very little. Her action of adultery is never denied. She does not ask for forgiveness from Jesus which is rather interesting, but nevertheless she receives it, not in the sense of a judicial decree but in a much deeper sense. She emerges from the story with a sense of being loved and cared for, with a sense of being cherished as a person, with a sense of being sent forth on a mission, with a sense of being connected, with a sense of being healed. All of that is present in her silence. The contrast between the pervasive guilt and condemnation that surround her in the beginning of the story when she is "brought" to Jesus like a convict, and the freedom in which she is portrayed at the end of the story when she is told to "go but sin no more," illustrates the voice of the woman who only speaks two words in the story.

Jesus himself is the agent of freedom. He acts here as he did with the Samaritan woman, in celebration of conscience. He responds first to the accusers, and then to the accused, and finally to the sin. By his presence he establishes the right order of things, for he loves both the accuser, the accused, and the law, but he keeps them in proper perspective. One of my former pastors, Monsignor Jim Coffey,[4] used to say that there are three realities that have to be kept in mind in living. They are God, man, and sin, and they must be kept in mind precisely in that order, or otherwise we end up with distortion. If we put sin first, then we have a terrible caricature of God as an avenger, as a monster, who exacts his ounce of flesh from humanity. If we put man first, then we have an inadequate concept of both God and sin and in the process man becomes dehumanized by being made either less or more than he is. If God is placed first, if he is in the center, then man can be man and sin can be sin without the reality of either being distorted. This is what Jesus appears to be doing in the story, and it can be shown through his approach to the accusers and the accused, for he approaches them out of a deep awareness of God's love for them, as the story shows.

Jesus responds first to the accusers, but his response to them, from one viewpoint anyway, is no different than his response to the woman. He approaches them with care and sensitivity. He knows that they are baiting him with a trap, and while he evades the trap, he does not react with hatred and violence, etc. He writes on the ground, but what he writes is undisclosed, yet its effect is enormous. It was of such strength as to cause those who were present to leave, beginning with the eldest. One can conjecture why the leave-taking begins with the eldest. He would have the longest lived history, the oldest memory, perhaps the most indiscretions. One can project what Jesus wrote. Was it their sins? Their offenses? Their names? The gospel allows us to fill in the blanks ourselves without itself being specific. What it does show is that Jesus was careful to maintain their anonymity, that he was not willing to expose them to the same ridicule or public condemnation and judgment that they had exercised in accusing the woman. He acted toward them with love, with sensitivity and with compassion. He even invited them to speak on their own behalf, which they did not ask of the woman. He said: "Let those without sin cast the first stone," an invitation that obviously brought them to the point of self-reflection.

Jesus was equally solicitous for the woman. When everybody left, he was alone with her. He could have lectured her, condemned her privately, etc., but there is no evidence of that. He treats her as a person rather than as an object, as a subject with her own lived experience, as a woman who is capable of and responsible for her own vision. He offers her forgiveness, and in this he energizes her so that she can separate herself from the sin. He refuses to judge her as others did, although it is clear that he does not condone the sin. He gives her back what had been taken from her, her self-respect and esteem. He is not motivated by punishment, but by concern, and so he frees her for her future rather than holding her in bondage to her past. She is called to confront the sin, to confront the reality of her life, and she is invited to move in a new direction. She is invited not to pass judgment on herself but on the act. There is a clear-cut question put to her: "Woman, has no one (including yourself) condemned you?" She said, "No one, Lord." And Jesus said, "Neither do I condemn you." It is only then that the reality of the sin is dealt with. Jesus says to her: "Go and do not sin again." Sin is in its place. The woman is restored to her place. She can, to use a phrase of Richard Gula, "lean into the future trustingly with the expectation that something good will happen."[5] They are both in their proper place precisely because God is in his—at the center.

I come home now to this story in prayer and try to see it in terms of a story of self. I go through the different steps, asking myself: What is the woman in me, and the Pharisees, etc.? For a long time the story didn't click, but then one day while I was reading it, I began to understand it as a story about real and false guilt, as a story about superego and conscience, as a story about a tension within me as I confront my own sinfulness. Many times as I reflect upon my life I come to an awareness that I have done something that is wrong; I have acted freely and knowingly in a way that has either destroyed or injured myself or others, that has in some way injured or hurt or harmed either myself or others as people. Sometimes it is an awareness that I have upset the order of life, that I have displaced God from his rightful position and elevated myself. In such instances I recognize my own sense of guilt and blame, and I recognize also my need to rectify the imbalances I have introduced through my behaviors into the order of things. Generally the recognition and correction of the disorder restores my sense of self-worth, self-esteem and peace. In a sense this is the meeting between the woman and Christ, between my sin and my conscience, between my bondage and freedom.

More frequently, however, there is another kind of meeting—the meeting between the woman and the Pharisees in me. Tom Kane has described this brilliantly in his book by identifying himself with the woman in the story and then using his imagination to amplify the image as she comes in contact with the Pharisees. Part of that meditation runs as follows: "The accusation of their (the Pharisees') eyes finds words, 'This woman has been caught in the act of adultery.' That action was unacceptable; she is unacceptable. I hear this accusation and ingest this vision of myself. I make it my own. I am guilty. That is my true reality. Welling up from my depths is a voice that accepts the verdict of my accusers. It is not that I have done something wrong, something shameful. I am wrong. This brooding sense, that all that I am is flawed, stained, overwhelms me. . . . I accept this terrible verdict of the Pharisees as true and I live under this intolerable burden."[6] I recognize that this is precisely what happens to me at times; it is exactly the way I feel, and the terror is that it is quite neurotic. I can and do feel this way at times even if there is no adultery, no precipitating action, nothing to "condemn" me for at all. The very accusation itself can trigger the response, expose the sense of guilt, intensify my feeling of rejection, deepen my sense of blame and suck me further into a strangling kind of depression. Even more sad is the feeling that because there is blame, guilt, exposure, confession, accusation, etc., the whole experience looks like confession, looks like a reconciliation is occurring but it is not a meeting between Christ and conscience, but between superego and ego, between the Pharisees and the woman.

Seen in this way, the story becomes revelatory for me. It enables me to become aware of different kinds of guilt and pseudo forgiveness that are present within me. It helps me to distinguish real and false guilt, the voice of conscience and superego, healthy and neurotic responses. It takes time to catch the tones of the different voices because they look so familiar initially. What Jesus does, however, is very different from what the Pharisees do. What Jesus does is invite the woman to commit, or recommit, her freedom to her future. What the Pharisees do is require and mandate her to surrender her freedom to her past. My question therefore becomes: How can I learn to distinguish these voices within me so that I can listen to the one and quiet the other, so that I can be attentive to that which helps me "lean trustingly into the future" and ignore that other voice of bondage?

John Glasser, S.J.[7] distinguishes the two voices along a number of planes and insists that the voice of superego produces unhealthy guilt while that of conscience brings about healthy guilt. He says that the former responds primarily to the insistence of "I should" while the latter dictates its path in terms of "I want." The former is motivated by a fear of loss of love and a need for approval, while the voice of conscience depends on the power of love to commit me because it sees the value of action or inaction in any situation. One of the principal differences between the two is that the superego voice tends to be static, repetitious, and compulsive. It cannot function creatively in a new situation while conscience remains sensitive to value in any situation and is therefore dynamic and innovative. In terms of after-effects, the voice of superego is punitive, it demands punishment, it exacts its ounce of flesh—the stoning of the woman—in its conviction that the punishment will effect the reconciliation. Conscience, on the other hand, seeks to restructure the future so that the perceived value may be pursued. "Go," says Jesus to the woman, "and sin no more." Ultimately, therefore, the voice of superego is a torture, a never-ending nagging sense that distorts our vision, corrupts our perceptions and relentlessly intensifies our bondage, forcing us to live out a life that increasingly feels more like a charade, while conscience acts within us as a source of motivation that encourages us to perceive and follow the deep values of life.

Looking at the story and reading it over and over, again and again, brings me home to these voices in me that have such strong effects upon my sense of self-worth and self-esteem, and that both act to demand reconciliation when they have been disobeyed. It makes me aware of how inept I am at really distinguishing these voices and at how adept I need to become so that I discover my future and my wholeness. My ability to do that enhances my capacity for choice. It will enable me to move more into that area of freedom that exists between guilt and sin, to accept my past with its failures, mistakes and indiscretions, my present with its imperfections and groping toward value, and my future which is constantly being opened to me from inside, instead of bombarding me from outside like some heavy burden I must shoulder to eternity.

Elizabeth Bowden Howes distinguishes between the psychological and the religious problem of forgiveness and tells us that the psychological problem is to search out and confront that which needs to be expiated, that which is "knotted and crossed and crooked in both the exterior and interior life." The religious problem she sees as bringing these into "the presence of God so that they may be accepted and reconciled and transformed." More importantly, she points out the danger of only going halfway, for, as she puts it, "if a man succeeds in opening up the negatives only for the purpose of getting them out, he is in danger of being possessed by them or of shutting them away again quickly because the pain of them is so great. If he sees them as indications of something new that wants to be born, accepted and loved, then he can permit them to be, holding them gently despite all their struggling until they can be quieted and changed."[8] This perhaps is the difference between the two voices of the story. The Pharisees only went halfway; they brought out the negative for, at best, the purpose of getting it out. Jesus, however, saw the woman, saw the struggle to be born, offered no condemnation, but held her gently in his loving eyes and offered her forgiveness into a future that was always hers.

Chapter 11
John 9:1—9:41
From Blindness to Sight

When I return to Ireland to visit my mother I am very aware of her failing eyesight and that now she is practically blind. She sees only shadows and outlines of things. I am also aware that I myself have reached that age in life where I find myself jostling distance glasses, reading glasses and sun glasses around with greater frequency. Perhaps it is these two factors that have made the next story John presents to us a rather strong one for me. It is not that he just presents to us one set of eyes, those of the blind man, but rather that he presents to us many sets of eyes in this story, each of them with different degrees of vision.

He sets the story at the end of the feast of Tabernacles where Jesus had proclaimed himself the light of the world, and now he follows that theme by having Jesus give light to darkened eyes, by giving sight to the blind man. However there is more than this going on in the story. Other people's eyes and vision are also affected. In fact as the blind man is coming into the light, so that he can see, others are moving into darkness. We shall explore and comment further on this in a moment.

The chapter itself follows the same structural pattern as that of the Samaritan woman story,[1] and there are also many similarities between this story and that of the paralyzed man in chapter 5[2] so that much of what we have said about these need not be repeated here. There are seven scenes in this chapter which we can list as follows:

vv 1–7   Healing of the blind man
vv 8–12   Neighbors question the man
vv 13–17   Pharisees question the man
vv 18–23   Pharisees question the parents
vv 24–34   Pharisees question the man again
vv 35–38   Jesus questions the man
vv 39–41   Pharisees question Jesus

As the scenes unfold and the story is told the blind man goes through a progressive widening of his vision. Initially we are told in v 7 that after the man washed in the pool of Siloam "he came back seeing." John carefully tells us that Siloam means "Sent," thereby exposing us to the double meaning since he has already said that Jesus was the one sent. What is it that the blind man sees at this point? John tells us in v 11 that he sees the *man* Jesus. By v 17, however, that vision has undergone a change. Now he sees that the person who cured him is a "prophet." In v 33 this vision deepens or widens. Now he sees someone who came from God because he could not do what he did otherwise. Finally in v 37 we are told that he confesses and believes that Jesus is the Son of Man.

While the blind man is undergoing this journey the Pharisees are going in the opposite direction. They see less and less. They are entering blindness. Initially in v 15 it appears that they accept the healing of the blind man. In v 17, however, they have moved rather subtly from the admission of this. Now they assert: "You *say* he opened your eyes." There appears to be some doubt about it. By v 24 they have taken a more obstinate position. Not only do they now doubt the miracle but they discredit the "miracle worker." They declare that Jesus is a sinner and therefore incapable of divine favor and blessing. By v 29 they completely deny his divinity by saying that they do not know where he comes from, and in v 34 they are ready to reject the blind man as well. They throw him out of the synagogue. The whole question of seeing and not knowing where he comes from reminds us of the meeting between the first disciples and Jesus that we commented on above.[3]

There is an interesting relationship suggested by these two progressive movements, one positive and the other negative, respectively. We notice that both groups make four statements in the process of their journey, and we print them here together for comparison purposes:

Blind Man	*Pharisees*
1. *v 12* I do not know (where Jesus is).	1. *v 16* The man who did this cannot be from God.
2. *v 25* I do not know if he (Jesus) is a sinner or not.	2. *v 24* We know this man is a sinner.
3. *v 36* Tell me who he is, sir (because I do not know).	3. *v 29* We know God spoke to Moses. We do not know where he comes from.
4. *v 38* I believe, Lord.	4. *v 34* You were born and raised in sin. Are you trying to teach us? They threw him out of the synagogue.

As we look at the two groups of statements we notice that the blind man's statements are all confessions of ignorance followed by a confession of faith. On the other hand the Pharisees' statements are all confessions of certainty leading to ignorance. Perhaps this structure itself conceals a message on the value of doubt, and the danger of certainty, in the matter of blindness and sight, and perhaps one could say that it also testifies to the old adage that sometimes our apparent vices are really our virtues and our apparent virtues are our real vices.

However, as I suggested above, these are not the only eyes in the story. There are other pairs of eyes worth noticing, like the parents' eyes. What is it they see in the story? Or the disciples' eyes—are they blind or are they light-filled? What about the man's neighbors? Where are they on the spectrum of sight and blindness? We have indicated that the Pharisees' eyes are going into progressive blindness. Is there anything that could account for their myopia? Then there is the blind man himself. What does he see? What drew him from the blindness? Jesus is the central figure in the story. What do his eyes see? And why is that liberating? All these questions form part of the structure and pattern of the story. John includes them all so that the reader will be awakened and come to sight through contact with the other multiple eyes of the story. I propose, therefore, to examine briefly what each of these pairs of eyes sees in the remainder of this chapter.

The first set of eyes we come upon are those of the disciples. These eyes see only a problem, and they see specifically a theological problem. Their question comes straight out of the Old Testament where, with some exceptions, suffering is thought to be the result of sin. The thing that catches my attention, however, is their failure to see the man. Their vision is one of abstraction. The eyes through which they perceive the person of the blind man are in this sense impersonal and limiting, reductive and prejudiced. They approach him with a set of assumptions, which in itself is understandable, but they appear to have difficulty going beyond those assumptions. They seem to have difficulty in allowing the blind man to speak for himself and to help them understand something about him. The person has given way to the problem, the man's predicament into a theological situation, and in the process the man himself gets lost. There is little interest in whether he is in pain, suffering, capable of being healed, etc. The man has become a case history.

These eyes are not unknown to me in my own life. As I look now at the disciples I am called to recognize the times when I approach others in a similar way. How frequently I see them in terms of "problems" or "cases." I become aware as I read the story of the way in which I talk of people as objects instead of as subjects. They become in those moments impersonal things, reduced to the less than human, by my eyes. I become aware of how easily and casually and even frequently I rob them of their subjectivity, and in the process I contaminate their freedom to be in charge of the project of their own existence. I begin to see through the eyes of the disciples my own attempts to have people validate my own theological predispositions in one way or another. I am called therefore by this aspect of the story to revisit and re-evaluate again the direction, process, and assumptions of my own caring, if I am to be assured that the light in me is not mainly darkness.

The second set of eyes that emerge in the story are very similar, except that they do not see a theological problem. In fact they do not all see the same thing. Some say: "He's the blind man." Others say: "He only looks like him." These eyes are essentially the eyes of the everyday. They see what they expect to see and don't quite believe anything that challenges that vision. They are conditioned eyes. Things must be the way they always were. Surprises are not expected or indeed welcomed. In this sense these eyes are also limiting and restraining.

The neighbors' eyes in me are easily activated whenever my security is threatened. These anxious eyes begin to twitch a little when the new and the unknown enters, when I anticipate the worst in any given situation and hand myself over to the anxiety and fear that is their way. In turn these eyes tend to limit and define my possibilities, narrow my horizons and call me back in caution from the challenge of the moment. They are also unrevealing eyes that prefer the initial barrier of distance to the risk of intimacy. But they are not always that way. Sometimes they see beyond the negative to the positive. Sometimes these eyes can be less serious and more relaxing. Sometimes they can laugh. They have two sides to them but they most often evidence themselves in the negative. They are filled with an anxious watchfulness, and if left to their own devices they can intoxicate and contaminate my vision.

The third set of eyes that emerge in the story are the eyes of the Pharisees. They look at the blind man and see not a problem but an opportunity. These are the eyes of certainty that believe that everything can be useful and turned into gain. Every adversity has its possibility. These eyes are controlled not by compassion, nor by care, nor by pain, but by power. These eyes try to impose their own vision on reality. They are able to ignore any and all evidence if necessary in pursuit of their own goal. In the story they move, as we notice, deeper and deeper into darkness until they can no longer see reality at all. They deny the cure, the miracle, the Christ, etc., etc. These eyes, controlled in one way by the desire for power, are controlled in another way by fear. Their eyes see the blind man's cure as a threat to their power and therefore their existence. Their eyes perceive Jesus as the power source of this threat, and so they are willing to get rid of the one (blind man) to eradicate the other (Jesus as power). In consequence they deny the cure and throw him out of the synagogue. These eyes are also the eyes of the guardians of life. They see themselves standing like Cerberus at the gates of Hades or the archangel Michael at the gates of paradise. They are protectors of the world of the sacred, and no entry is possible other than through their pre-determined approval and sanction.

Within my own life these eyes are often the most difficult to see. They are eyes of certainty filled with blindness, eyes of power filled with weakness, eyes of protection filled with vulnerability; but in each case the second part is ignored. In the story the Pharisees try to stand between the blind man and Jesus. These eyes of theirs function like that within me. They are the defense structures that at one time were necessary to my life. They enabled me to grow and develop. Now they have become ingrained and their vision is blindness. They guard, protect, stand in the way of, prevent, etc., the connection with the self. These eyes are the most obstinate eyes within, the hardest to move, the least willing to compromise. They are by now the eyes of my habitual way of being and seeing, that operate in the persistency of routine, and so are engrained in my very character itself. To become conscious of their existence is already for me to begin to turn away from the blindness with which they overtake me and return again to sight.

The fourth set of eyes in the story of the blind man are those of the parents. These eyes are rather ambiguous. On the one hand the eyes see what has happened to their son. They cannot and do not deny that he has been healed. They do not deny either that he was blind, "We know that he is our son. We know that he was born blind. But we do not know how it is that he can now see. Ask him. He is old enough." In this sense the eyes are delighting eyes, but the story shows us a second side when it says that they "said this because they were afraid of the Jewish authorities who had already agreed that anyone who professed Jesus was the Messiah would be put out of the synagogue." There is a restriction to their ability to delight in their son's sight. They are frightened eyes as well, and they are caught between fear and delight. They are continually aware of where the source of power is, and it is outside them. They are continually aware of who is watching them, listening to them, and paying attention to them.

These eyes are self-conscious eyes. Sam Keen comments in another context that "when I am self-conscious (as opposed to self-aware) it is really someone else's eyes who are watching, judging, criticizing me. And I always fail to come up to the standard of the watcher. . . . Watchers are the prosecuting attorney in the court of infantile experience."[4] There is both strength and weakness in these eyes. Their strength resides in the awareness that they have of their love for their son and their responsiveness to that love. They are aware of their love and yet of the limitations of that love. They are unwilling to accept a responsibility that appropriately belongs somewhere else. This is reflected in their redirecting the Pharisees to their son: "Ask him. He is old enough and he can answer for himself." The weakness of these eyes is in their inability to go beyond that love to "the love that moves the sun and all the other stars."[5] They are held back by the fear that weighs them down.

I find that these parental eyes are also alive within me. How frequently I act and, in the very moment of disposing of myself in action, discover that I am, subtly or otherwise, watching to discover what others think. "To be is to be

seen" seems to be my motto at such moments. It prevents
true spontaneous play, the real laughter in the eyes, the little madness that Zorba tells the boss man he lacks. I still
only exist as a reflection of others around me to whom I
give authority. Their fears and anxieties I permit to limit my
freedom, their opinions and thought condition my judgment, their prisons and limitations condition my existence.
In such moments I leave the attentiveness to what is before
my eyes and go hunting after an illusion, even though I
know that "people who think effectively will use their powers of attention, intelligence and reason in an integrated
fashion."[6] I don't exactly deny the miracle of my own decision, I don't exactly deny the value of my own vision, I
don't exactly abort the choice of my own emerging humanity, but I don't go beyond the love I have received as a child
to the "love that moves the sun and all the stars" and wants
to love me into freedom. I remain, as Keen said, "self-
unconsciously focused inward in the court of conscience,
vainly trying to present [my] case in a good light so [I] can
get a verdict of not guilty."[7]

The fifth set of eyes in the story belong to the blind
man himself. What is it that these eyes see? When he was
blind he was unable to see. Grady says that he was in a
state of non-relation, an I–it situation.[8] Now, however, he
is in a state of relationship. He sees someone loving him,
caring for him, nurturing him to freedom. He sees eyes that
do not judge him and do not limit him. He sees eyes that
do not condemn him to his past but seek his future. These
eyes of the blind man are the truly delighting eyes. They
delight in the one who loves him and who has freed him.
These eyes will not be seduced. They speak of good news,
they witness, they proclaim. These eyes tell a story. They
are open. They do not understand everything. There is
much they cannot comprehend in terms of how and why,

etc., but they are open to further discovery. "Tell me who he is, sir, so that I can believe in him." These eyes begin to make connections that are credible. "Since the beginning of time it has never been heard that someone opened the eyes of a man born blind." These eyes are the eyes of simplicity and wonder. They are receptive and they are humble. "I don't know if he is a sinner or not. One thing I do know: I was blind and now I see." They are also resolute. They see Christ even if they do not recognize him in his totality. They sense that the person who addresses them is from God, and in the knowledge of that they can endure questioning, ridicule, embarrassment and even excommunication from the synagogue if necessary. These eyes are at last connected and know that the connectedness can be trusted. The irony of the story is important to remember here, and it is this: the person in the darkness comes to sight; those with sight go to darkness. There is a connection between the person's darkness and his sight.

I find these eyes within me in moments of meditation. In those moments one must first become stilled, must first enter the dark, become quiet. In these moments the ordinary way of seeing only leads to blindness. Here the process of thinking, analyzing, working, introspection, etc., are quieted, and a way opens up that is best described as a give and take, an exchange. The loss of the ordinary way of functioning is experienced as a kind of blindness initially but gradually in the darkness something begins to happen and I learn to see in a new way. I am no longer self-conscious about my blindness, or particularly concerned about others' views, or trying to figure out the power possibilities in every moment. I am neither in time past or time future, only in time present, and in this time I begin to see, without understanding, without thought, and indeed without love, but, as T. S. Eliot says, "There is faith,"[9] and it is with faith that I see. I connect with something deep within me, an inkling, a dream, a symbol, a story, a self. Something comes into my—or out of my—darkness, and as I attend to it, I begin to see.

The sixth set of eyes in the story of the blind man belong to Christ. What is it that these eyes see? This eye is the eye of the contemplative. Jesus sees the person. He sees what God sees. They see all that there is and nothing less. They see totally and not partially; therefore they see the heart beyond behavior. These eyes are the eyes of acceptance. They accept the blind man on his own terms and do not judge him in terms of carrying the weight of other eyes. They see him as person and not scapegoat, as individual and not collective, as unique and not machine product. The man's blindness has nothing to do with his sins or his parents' sins. These eyes see "God's power at work," and because they do they know the way out of the blind man's blindness. They can give the clues: "Go and wash in the pool of Siloam." These eyes reveal God. They speak and say: "You have seen him; he is the one who is talking to you now." These eyes are mirrors, for they return to the gazer the eyes they turn toward him, and so you have as in a mirror an inverse situation: blind eyes see, and seeing eyes are blind. These eyes turn life upside down and then turn it around again. Peter Mann, writing of Christ as communicator, says that he had the ability to "disorient people in order to reorient them . . . inviting them to a new way of thinking, feeling, and seeing . . . [so that the] reign of God's unbounded love, peace, justice and wholeness . . . becomes their goal."[10] That is what these eyes do in this story. They disorient in turn the blind man's eyes, the Pharisees' eyes, the parents' eyes, the disciples' eyes, so that they can reorient them, and in the process they disorient the seventh set of eyes that we shall meet, which are the eyes of the reader who by that very act is also in the story.

The eyes of Christ are also within me. They are the eyes of the totality of the self that manifest themselves to me in myths and stories, in symbols and dreams. They know the way to wholeness and offer a way out of the dilemmas of life. Initially they disorient, sometimes even frighten, but this "disorientation is for the sake of reorientation." They come as gift and point me in the direction of wholeness. They confront me with a light that is experienced as blindness, or, to put it another way, these eyes reveal the blindness and, in seeing, accepting and integrating what it reveals, one draws closer to wholeness. Jung says that "he who is truly and hopelessly little will always drag the revelation of the greater down to the level of his littleness, and will never understand that the day of his littleness has dawned. But the man who is inwardly great will know that the long expected friend of his soul, the immortal one, has come to lead captivity captive, that is, to seize hold of him with whom this immortal had always been confined and held prisoner and to make his life flow into that greater life."[11]

The last or seventh set of eyes in the story of the blind man are the eyes of the reader. Culpepper has indicated that in these times the term "reader" must be further refined as we learn to distinguish such things as "intended readers, implied readers, historical readers, model readers, mock readers, ideal readers."[12] All of these, of course, have their eyes, and as they read their eyes enter the story. What I mean by the "eyes of the reader" is all of these in a general sense, but the meditative reader in a particular sense. The meditative reader brings to the story his own life with all of its strengths and weaknesses because he wants to receive the vision of the story by handing himself over to it. The eyes of the reader are the eyes that want to be, expect to be, hope to be changed by this contact. These eyes are the eyes that want to see the new vision projected by the images. They are the eyes that are willing to risk the transformation of life. In the process of the transformation we come to see that all the eyes of the story are our own eyes and that in the course of reading the story we encounter the "one, protean, multidimensional, mysterious self that we are as we go through the different permutations of the self. We encounter the different eyes within ourselves that reveal us to be victims and healers, sacred and demonic, blind and seeing."[13]

Chapter 12
John 10:1—10:41
From Outside to Inside

We have mentioned previously how John is circling the great Jewish feasts, recalling them to mind and then having Jesus replace or fulfill them. Thus he has presented Jesus as Lord of the sabbath, as the real bread from heaven that celebrates Passover, as the real Torah and Wisdom of God who is himself the living Water and the Light of the world. Now he comes to the last great liturgical feast which in many ways was associated with the feast of Tabernacles. It is the feast of Dedication.

The feast itself is known by many names.[1] Since it was celebrated in December it is sometimes called the feast of Chislev. Josephus called it the feast of lights because of the prominent place they played in the processions, etc., while the rabbis themselves seemed to prefer the name Hanukkah, the name by which it is best known today.

The feast has its origin in the Old Testament. During the year 167 B.C. the Jews were persecuted by Antiochus IV who destroyed their temple, forbade them to celebrate their feasts and ordered them to give up their customs, tradition and culture. In short he tried to destroy their Jewishness. His goal was to unify the people of his kingdom through uniformity of thought, word, action and worship. To this end he built a new altar to Zeus at which he expected the people to worship. Some people did, and in particular two of these are worth mentioning, Jason and Menalaus, because they were of high-priestly rank. Three years later Judas Maccabeus reversed this disastrous state of affairs. He erected a new altar to Yahweh, rededicated the temple and the people to God and offered sacrifice. There was great rejoicing over this and so a celebration was established which in the course of time became an annual event. It was characterized by processions with palms, the singing of the Hallel, and the use of lights.

It is this feast that acts as background to chapter 10 of the gospel. Certainly by v. 22 Jesus is already at this feast. Many commentators see the introductory vv. 1–21 as a connecting bridge uniting the feasts of Dedication and Tabernacles. Brown[2] says that in these verses John is looking backward to the feast of Tabernacles and forward to the feast of Dedication. The image of the Good Shepherd dominates the chapter, but it has two subsidiary images worth mentioning first, i.e., the images of the gateway and the sheep.

The Gateway: In drawing attention to the sheepfold and the gate John is drawing on the conditions of his own time and utilizing as a metaphor a practice that existed among the people. Apparently there were two kinds of shepherds in Palestine. There were the herdsmen who would stay out in the fields, out in the open, among the hills, at night. These are probably the shepherds referred to in the infancy narrative. There was a second group that used to bring their

flocks home in the evening. Sometimes a number of shepherds would bring their flocks together and keep them
together during the night.

In order to protect these sheep, this second group of
shepherds, who are probably the ones referred to in chapter
10, would build a pen or corral to hold the flock. This was
generally in the form of a stone wall fence which circled the
flock and had an opening or gate that permitted the shepherd to enter. During the night, especially if a number of
herds were kept together, a watchman or "keeper" would
sit at this gate. He would allow only those he knew and
trusted the right of entry to the flock. In the morning each
of the shepherds would come and enter through this gate
and lead his sheep out to pasture. They would recognize his
voice and come out after him. The wall therefore was essentially a defensive structure designed to keep the flock
together and to protect the sheep. Without it they would
easily scatter and the life of the flock would be endangered.
In this way then the shepherd strove to protect the integrity
and life of his flock.

The gateway is an important part of the image. It is the
way into the flock. The one who goes through the gate is
recognized by the keeper who opens for him and by the
sheep who recognize him. He stands in contrast to any others who approach the flock in a different manner. What is
being stressed in and through the image of the gate is the
method of approach, the process, the correct manner, the
way to enter the sheepfold while respecting the integrity of
the flock, and the necessity of, and the importance of, the
defensive structure. The words that are used to describe the
shepherd's entry into the fold all imply respect, watchfulness, understanding, etc. They are in contrast to the method
and purpose of entry of those who enter the fold in any
other manner.

In stressing that he is the gateway Jesus is drawing attention to emergence. This can be observed by noting that if he spoke of the wall or the pen he would be talking more of the protective aspect. The gate expresses the function of openness, allowing one into the fold for the purpose of leading them out, for their own sake. It is true that a gate also closes and houses what is within, that it can keep it locked up and imprisoned. That, however, does not appear to be the sense in which it is used here.

The Sheep: John quickly moves from the first image to the second image in which he begins to accent the responsiveness of the sheep to the different entrants. From the process of entry he begins to move to the effect of entry. He speaks of the sheep which is itself an interesting image. The word tends to imply a flock or a multitude more than an individual sheep. They are the crowd animal, the collective animal, one could say, who is easily affected and influenced by the leading ram. The sheep tend to lose their individuality and to act as a group. In this regard it is interesting to see how John points to the shepherd's knowledge of the individual. He leads them out as individuals, calling each by name and allowing them to be pastured individually while remaining part of the group. The sheep respond positively to this action, and there is a mutuality affected between them and the shepherd. They know each other.

The sheep respond differently to those who do not respect the process of entry. Those who violate the defensive structure of the flock and who enter the fold in another manner are described as strangers, hired hands, thieves, robbers and marauders. This is in itself an image of progressive deterioration and violence. It portrays an image of total lack of interest in either the individual sheep or the welfare of the group. Not only does such a person affect the sheep negatively but he himself is affected by his own lack of care and respect. The purpose of this person's entry to the sheepfold is also described in violent terms. He comes to steal, to slaughter and to destroy. The sheep respond to this treatment negatively. They do not recognize such a person. They will not follow; they will scatter and run away. The flock will be further torn apart and disintegrated.

The Shepherd: The shepherd is, as we indicated, the third image, and that image dominates the chapter. In the foregoing we have already said much about the shepherd but more needs to be said. Many of us have formed our images of shepherds on the basis of picture postcards which portray nice farming communities in rather idyllic mountain settings. Usually the scene is peaceful and quiet, with plenty of light, fresh water and meadows, etc. These images, however, tend not to reflect the biblical image of the shepherd which is quite ambivalent.

In the Old Testament the image appears first as a rather positive one. Moses was accepted as a shepherd. Kings are frequently referred to as shepherds even though they were never formally given the title. Yahweh himself is referred to as the Shepherd, and in his care the people shall not want but shall walk with him even through the valley of darkness. In all of these images the shepherd is a rather positive figure who is seen to nurture and care for the flock.

There is, however, a second side where they are not seen in such a noble light. Jeremiah is very tough on them and faults them "for their failure to meet their responsibilities" (Jer 2:8). He calls them "stupid" (Jer 10:21), and accuses them of scattering the flock (Jer 23:1) and of "leading the people astray" (Jer 50:6). In Ezekiel they are further described as being unfaithful and having no understanding (Ez 34:2,10).

Kenneth Bailey[3] goes even a little further by pointing to the reality of shepherds in John's and Jesus' time, saying that "flesh and blood shepherds who in the first century wandered around after sheep were clearly unclean . . . and any man who believed that shepherds were unclean would naturally be offended if addressed as one." The shepherd, he maintains, is not a very favorable title, and he suggests that in claiming the title (in Luke) Jesus is identifying himself with the outcasts, the despised and the rejected.

John has Jesus collapse the ambiguity by claiming: "I am the Good Shepherd." Painter[4] notes that while in the synoptics the word "good" is frequently used of fruit, works, trees, ground, need, pearls, fish, circumstances, salt and measure, in John it is used only of wine, the Shepherd, and the works. Good in this sense means the proper fulfillment of a function, which is perhaps why some prefer the translation "model shepherd." Jesus is for John fulfilling his proper function, and John develops that for us in two ways: (1) by contrasting him with the hired hand, and (2) by enunciating the qualities that the shepherd possesses.

1. We have already seen the contrast between the shepherd and the outsiders, marauders, strangers, etc. The hired hand, however, is an insider. He is part of the shepherd's family. Here he is envisaged negatively as one who only works for money, who does not care for the sheep, who does not establish a relationship with them and who readily abandons them. These are the shepherds that Ezekiel in ch. 34 condemns as not caring for the flock. Instead they plundered it, neglected it, fed themselves on it, but they have not pastured it, which for him means they have not strengthened the weak, healed the sick or brought back the strayed. John says that they see the wolf coming and they take flight, leaving the flock unprotected. Jesus is a Shepherd in contrast to this kind of shepherding. He is the Good Shepherd.

2. Jesus exhibits the positive qualities of the Good Shepherd. He establishes a relationship to the flock. He knows them and they know him. He recognizes them in their individuality. He will lead them out to where they will be appropriately fed. He will protect them. He will do even more. He will lay down his life. He will become himself the sacrifice and the altar. He will dedicate himself for them. This shepherd has come for their sake, he is free to lay down his life for them, and he will do that because he cares. This shepherd is leader, guide, revealer, nourisher and caretaker. This is an "I am" statement, and it is consistent with what we said about them in chapter 8 above, for here Jesus is saying who he is for them.

In 10:22–30, the picture changes and now we are at the feast of the Dedication. The Jews want to know if he is the Messiah, and, as at Tabernacles, there is again the charge of blasphemy, the attempt to stone him, the growing hostility. Brown points out that there are two questions: "Is Jesus the Messiah?" and "Does he make himself God?"[5] It ends with Jesus going even further than he has gone before. He says that he and the Father are one. We have watched this developing throughout the gospel. He is first of all the Word of the Father. Then he tells us that his life is fulfilling the Father's will, that he not only sees what the Father is doing but he does what the Father does, and that he speaks only what he has heard from the Father. Now he presents himself as the gate through which the flock can go, as the Shepherd who leads them, as the one who lays down his life for them, and finally he says to them: "The Father and I are one." No one can snatch the sheep out of his hand and no one can snatch the sheep out of his Father's hand. There is here, as Brown says, a "unity of power and operation."[6] Jesus is the Good, Model, Dedicated Shepherd who is willing to offer his life in sacrifice for his sheep.

There is here also a reference to the dedication cere-

monies. In each of the other feasts to which we have
referred, Jesus is perceived as replacing the event in question, but here Jesus proclaims that he is consecrated by God.
This is meant to awaken the memory we referred to earlier
when we spoke of the ceremonies dedicating and consecrating the new temple. Jesus therefore is for John here
claiming to be the new tabernacle and the new temple. He
is, says Schillebeeckx, "the new sanctuary, the altar consecrated by God himself; he gives freedom to those who live
in slavery among the nations; he gives eternal life (10:28)—
God's presence among us."[7]

I come to the story now in prayer and let my eye wan-
der over each of its elements—the sheep, the pen, the
intruders, the shepherd—and as I do so I gradually become
aware of their presence in me and how the story is opening
me to newness and to wholeness. I find myself asking what
are the sheep in my life now. Where is the crowd side of
my identity dominating my existence? How and in what
ways am I merely the institutional man, the company man,
the unreflective voice of the herd? I find myself thinking
about the difference of the sheep locked into the pen and
the sheep when they are led out to grazing beyond the con-
fines and strictures of the defensive structures. How is the
wholeness of my life different when I am unconsciously
bonded with a viewpoint or a position or a feeling of the
group and when I choose consciously such a position or
relationship. I wonder about the pen in my life and see it in
this story not so much in the neurotic defense mechanism I
have evolved in my life as in what we might call the character defenses that I have formed in my everyday living.
What, I find the pen asking of me, are the routines and pat-
terns of my life that at one time helped me to adapt to life
but that now stand in the way of further growth? What is
the most obstinate tendency that I am aware of and that I

cling to now as a conscious source of strength? Is it my striving for power or perfection or knowledge, etc.?

The wolf I find begins to attract my attention, and I see it in the story as a source of danger. I realize that in myth and stories the wolf can either be the friend or the enemy of people, that, as Helen Luke observes in her commentary on the *Divine Comedy*, "he is often the most despised and feared of beasts, in fact and in legend; [he] is also the most honored. Those who know him well tell of his intelligence and noble qualities, of his loyalty to the death, giving the lie to his evil reputation. In myth and in fact he alone will adopt and nourish a human child."[8] While the wolf has both positive and negative qualities here, it is the negative side that dominates. What, therefore, is the wolf in my life? Marian Woodman, who does a lot of work with patients with eating disorders, describes what she calls the "wolf attitude" as the "attitude which demands more and more and more by day and howls 'I want' at night,"[9] and a little later, quoting Marie L. Von Franz, says: "It represents the strange indiscriminate desire to eat up everybody and everything."[10] That is just the way the wolf functions in the story, and it brings to my attention my own appetites for food, sex, attention, love, work, drink, pleasure, etc. How are my appetites dealing with my life or how am I dealing with these appetites and what needs to happen?

What is the door to freedom and the future, the avenue to wholeness and completeness, and where is the Shepherd manifesting in my life? Where is the friend that is guide and revealer who knows and calls the collective me forward? The door itself is the opening, the avenue or, perhaps better still, the "threshold" to the future. It is the point of breakthrough, the place of exit and entry. Is there a place like that in my life that bridges the conscious and unconscious, that becomes the way in for the shepherd self and the way out for the sheep? I think of it now as my "dreams," the doorway to the unconscious and the avenue to the future, the break in the defense system, that place in my psychic life where I can both know and be known, wherein I meet the Shepherd who, though he is not the Father, is one with the Father and speaks only what he hears, who comes that I may have life and have it to the full.

Chapter 13
John 11:1—12:8
From Death to Life

One evening recently I was watching television when the title of a show attracted me. It was called The Lazarus Syndrome. Subsequently I discovered that it was not just one show but the title of a whole series. The series concerned itself with describing and portraying different attitudes and responses to life and death. The particular evening I watched was focused around a doctor's fears, frustrations and beliefs when he had to confront the fact that in spite of his best efforts some of his patients die. It portrayed the expectations placed on the medical profession by the community at large and how they sometimes unconsciously buy into the image. Other episodes I gather examine the conflict between doctor and priest in regard to what to say to a "terminally ill patient," and between doctors and families, etc. In a sense that is what this chapter is about. John sets out to deal with some attitudes prevalent in his own community and the surrounding culture in regard to death.

Exegetes[1] point out that this story is unique to John. There are some stories with similar characteristics found in the synoptics, e.g. Mark 11:11 where we are informed that Jesus stayed at Bethany on his trips to Jerusalem, and Luke 10:38 which refers to the home and hospitality of Martha and Mary but makes no reference to Lazarus. Whether the families of these stories and that of John are the same or different still remains in dispute, but many authorities claim that they are the one family.

In either case John treats this family as an important part of his gospel message, and his introduction of them at this juncture of his story is no mere accident. He has been insisting on the need for decision in regard to Christ.[2] He has allowed, and in fact fostered, the crisis between belief and unbelief throughout the gospel. Here now, as Jesus reveals himself as the life-giver, the need for that decision becomes even more important. Following this sign event some will grow more hostile and violent and join the ranks of those plotting to kill him; others will follow. The lines of demarcation between the two become clearer, the gulf widens, the inevitability of the final clash becomes apparent.

Structurally the chapter can be seen in terms of a flow of energy, moving from Mary, who gets all the attention initially, to Martha, who quickly takes on a leading role to the confrontation at the tomb between the dead Lazarus and the life-giving Jesus. It can also be seen in terms of a more dialectical structure as Crossan suggests.[3] He sees it in terms of a series of seven dialogues in which the fourth dialogue acts as the centerpoint of the story. Viewed from this vector the story focuses on the confrontation between the Jews and Jesus, and the central statement of the chapter then becomes the proclamation of the Jews, "See how Jesus loved him," which is an announcement of the truth and a description of the way things are in reality.

Martha occupies a large portion of this story. Whether in the Lukan or the Johannine stories she has been perceived frequently to be the activist who is busy about many things. In many ways she receives rather poor press from those who reflect on her presence. Elizabeth Bowden Howes, for instance, sees her as one who "wants to please, to have everything just right . . . perhaps not just to seek the approval of Jesus but to meet her own standards of perfection."[4] In a similar vein Arturo Paoli says that Jesus' comment is not brought on by the collection of plates and casseroles but by the fact that Martha has not yet found the other, she has not yet gone into the depths. . . . Her self is still exteriorized; it is looking for security, joy, shelter . . . and therefore, necessarily, even though she does not want to, she uses, instrumentalizes, thingifies; she does not accept. . . . Martha clings, whether she dominates or is submissive, even though she does not know it consciously."[5]

Not all, however, see her in such a negative way. Schnackenburg says that she is presented as a woman prepared to believe, "who, in a form deliberately kept general and indefinite, indicates a hope, and expresses a request which leaves all possibilities open."[6] In terms of her presence here for John, I believe that she expresses the faith of Judaism and the Jewish culture. She reflects the Jewish attitude toward death that John was trying to counteract in his own community. She expresses the faith that Lazarus will rise again on the last day, which for her means at the end of time, at the end of the ages. In this she is the representative voice of the collectivity of Israel. She is their spokesperson. It is this viewpoint that Jesus challenges. He is not offering salvation at some future time but right now, at this moment. Kysar offers the following observation: "Christianity was probably born amid a belief that the salvation of humanity lay in the future, and that that future was very near. What John does is move it into the present."[7] Martha is being invited to revise some of her views regarding life and death. She is being asked not if she accepts and consents to some intellectual proposition but rather if she accepts and believes in the bonding between Jesus and her in the moment that is now. The point that Jesus is making is that resurrection is not some vague hope for a future time but that it is a present experience.

Martha's answer to this invitation is crucial for John. It is little wonder then that for him she becomes the great proclaimer of faith. Here it is a woman and not a man, it is Martha and not Peter, who makes the outstanding profession of faith. It is she who says, "You are the Christ, the Son of the living God." This kind of affirmation of faith is totally unexpected and therefore all the more powerful a testimony and credible to the attuned listener. Schüssler Fiorenza says that "whereas in the original miracle source the raising of Lazarus stood at the center of the story the evangelist has placed the dialogue and confession of Martha at the center of the whole account. . . . As a beloved disciple of Jesus she is the spokeswoman for the whole Messianic faith of the community. . . . Her confession parallels that of Peter. . . . It has the full sense of the Petrine confession at Caesarea Philippi. Thus Martha represents the apostolic faith of the Johannine community just as Peter did for the Matthean community."[8] Martha moves to bond with Jesus. Her faith motivates her to accept the relationship that was offered to her in the present moment as she meets and confronts the one who has the life-giving power associated with the last days and the end of all things.

In fact the importance of Martha for John can be perceived in another way. He presents us, for those who like the "Sevens Theory," with seven women in his gospel, and significantly Martha is the fourth.

- In chapter 2 the ministry begins with Mary who intervenes with Jesus on behalf of a couple.
- In chapter 4 the disciples are shocked at Jesus' conversing with a woman but through it ministry extends to Gentiles.
- In chapter 8 in a later insertion into the gospel, a woman is presented whose presence necessitates Jesus' choice to move to the cross.
- In chapter 11 Martha articulates the correct Christology in her faith profession.
- In chapter 12 Mary demonstrates the right praxis of discipleship in her anointing of Jesus.
- In chapter 19 four women stand at the cross with the beloved disciple in a new community of brothers and sisters.
- In chapter 20 Mary Magdalene is the first disciple to receive a resurrection appearance.[9]

While the gospel story gives some material to work on in the case of Martha, it appears to be rather quiet about Mary. No less a scholar than Raymond Brown tells us that her presence "does not advance the action and that verse 34 could easily follow verse 27 and no one would notice the difference."[10] Because of this her presence has frequently been seen in terms of a contrast. Schnackenburg says that her presence allows John "to compare and contrast the attitude of the two sisters and traditionally she has been perceived as the contemplative over against Martha's activism."[11] Elizabeth Bowden Howes goes so far, in her comments on the two sisters in Luke, as to suggest that the two sisters "treat Jesus in totally opposite ways and receive opposite reactions from him." Martha, therefore, she sees as a complaining woman whose "compulsive existence has her caught in a pattern of egocentricity," while Mary is "centered on the creative value." She has chosen, says Bowden Howes, and it is that choice that is important.[12]

John himself introduces Mary to us as the "one who poured the perfume on the Lord's feet and wiped them with her hair." This story he later relates in chapter 12. It is a story that in one form or another appears in all four gospels, although there are some significant differences in the telling of the story by the different authors. Critics believe that the story recorded by John is the same as that recorded by Matthew 26:6–13 and Mark 14:3–11 but different from that recorded by Luke 7:36–38. Nevertheless, as the *Jerome Biblical Commentary* points out, it does appear that the "Johannine version of the anointing is the result of a combination of details from the narratives of Luke and Matthew–Mark."[13]

It is the importance of this anointing itself, however, that captured my attention. Why should John so carefully refer to it in the story of Lazarus? Jesus admonishes Judas, in the story of the anointing, because he complains about the extravagance of the event, the cost of the oil, the wasting of it, etc. Jesus points out to him that the purpose of the anointing was to prepare Jesus for burial, a point that is even more emphatically stated by Mark when he says, "She has done what she could: she has anointed my body beforehand for burial" (Mark 14:8). Schüssler Fiorenza sees in this evidence that "Mary is the true disciple and ministers to Jesus in contrast to the betrayer who was one of the twelve." She contends therefore that "while Martha of Bethany is responsible for the primary articulation of the community's Christological faith, Mary of Bethany articulates the right praxis of discipleship."[14] Mary's action in anointing Jesus' body is a prophetic action and it reflects her acceptance of Jesus' death at least at some level of her existence.

The third member of the family is Lazarus who has tended to be the one given the most attention. It is unusual for John to give a name to any of the characters whom Jesus meets in the sign stories. They are kept anonymous—the Samaritan woman, the blind man, etc. Lazarus, however, is named. His very name is significant. It means whom God helps. We are told that he was sick and that the news of his illness was brought to Jesus. Jesus does nothing for two days, which is a little surprising in view of the fact that we are specifically told that he loved Lazarus. John, however, makes this non-action of Jesus deliberate so that he can go on and point out that Lazarus was dead by the time Jesus got to the tomb four days later. To establish the point further, he even has reference to the smell of the decayed flesh; further, when the disciples misunderstand Jesus' reference to the fact that Lazarus is asleep, and that he will wake him, then John has Jesus say plainly to them, "Lazarus is dead."

Why this emphasis? Why does Lazarus, a dead man, form the center-point of the story? John has carefully structured it because he wants to indicate that this sickness of Lazarus, this death, is purposive. The sickness will not end in death, but rather in manifesting God's glory. Through the sign event he shows once again Jesus as life-giver. He has power over death. When he calls Lazarus from the tomb and in response Lazarus comes out, his hands and feet wrapped in grave cloths, and a cloth around his face, Jesus told them to untie him and let him go free. Then we have a clear and unmistakable sign that Jesus can give eternal life. He can give life that will not be destroyed by death.

At the tomb Jesus himself, we are told, is deeply moved. Jesus is affected. He sees Mary and those with her weeping, and he himself weeps. This is an important moment in John because it is one of those places where we touch Jesus' humanity. John is always anxious to protect the divinity of Jesus, and so he tends to underscore much of his human limitations and we will see a great deal of evidence of this in dealing with the passion narrative. Here we touch the humanness of Jesus, his connectedness to the earth. Many commentators attribute the weeping to the feeling and the love he had for Lazarus. The Jews themselves do so in the story, and yet maybe there is a different understanding available. Culpepper suggests that "the pattern of emotions indicates that it is the approach of his own death which moved Jesus."[15] Taken all in all, one could wonder if this is not John's version of Gethsemani where Jesus in the presence of Lazarus has to do battle with his own oncoming death.

The miracle of the raising of Lazarus has an immediate effect. By a strange coincidence it brings about his own death. The Sanhedrin gather together and become more actively involved in plotting his destruction. Their hostility becomes more conscious. The leaders plan to bring him to trial, to judgment, and to death. Others join them. Some follow Jesus. The plans for his death, however, turn out to be his path to glory and his return to the Father. We have here another example of the great irony of John who now shows us Jesus being condemned to death for giving life to Lazarus. In his meeting with this family Jesus has called them to re-examine their own attitude to life and death, and at the same time John shows us in "exaggeratedly simple terms, admittedly bordering on allegorization, Martha representing the ideal of discerning faith and service, Mary (representing) unlimited love and devotion and Lazarus (representing) the hope of resurrection life."[16]

The story comes alive to me in prayer and it invites me to consider death, not only in general but also in particular. Through Martha it asks me to identify the cultural trends and responses in my own time to death; through Mary it asks me in what way I accept my own death; through Lazarus it calls me to identify what part of me is dead and in the tomb; through Jesus it asks me to come to life again.

My own time is characterized by many as a death culture. Death and the fear of death seem to be present everywhere. Around us there is an abortion mentality, an euthanasia mentality, etc. We feel the pressure of the nuclear holocaust on every side and deliberate upon the fantasy of surviving a nuclear war. Claims and counterclaims of its effect upon the minds of children and adults are made. Death is in the air. Ecologists speak and inform us that conditions for human life may disappear within the next twenty to forty years. Death is in the land. Artists and poets speak and tell us that we are dialoguing with the absurd. Death is in the mind.

The culture, however, not only speaks its fear and its conviction that death is everywhere but it offers us its response, and in many cases it is horrific. In New Jersey three children commit suicide; in New York we read of a suicide-murder pact; in Chicago someone jumps from a window. The reality of the response matches the images we have read in Dostoyevsky's story of Kirilov in *The Possessed* who hopes to liberate mankind from his fear of death through his own suicide or in Camus' *Caligula* who sees the answer in terms of a "superior suicide." So now we witness all around us the need and existence of suicide prevention centers and we can read of a modern author who writes at the beginning of his work that "sooner or later everyone becomes a survivor of someone else's suicide."[17] It appears that this is at least part of our culture's answer—to say to us that suicide is the way out. Death is the answer to death; and I breathe in that answer with many images I see on television, with the books I read, with the music I hear, with the scientific reports I glance at, until it becomes a familiar answer that tends to become part of me and I wonder: Is it the answer?

It is not that the answer is a purely intellectual one. I have lived with someone who found in suicide some kind of answer. I have counseled with a woman who told me she would kill herself, and despite the best medical help we could get for her she ended up "gassing" herself to death in an automobile. I have over the course of twenty years in ministry been called to anoint both children and adults who have hanged themselves, shot themselves, jumped in front of trains, and overdosed. The "cultural" response has summoned me both intellectually and experientially to ask if suicide is the answer to the death that seems to surround us. If in the story Martha articulates the Jewish cultural response to death, then the Martha in me that articulates suicide as part of the cultural response of our time is now challenged by Jesus. I reject it again as I have before, and I accept that life is now, that eternal life is offered in the moment that is now.

Death is nevertheless a reality. It still is present. How then shall I prepare to meet it? Should I respond like Yeats in "Under Ben Bulben" and "cast a cold eye on life and death"[18] or like Dylan Thomas who advises his father not "to go gently into that good, good night" but rather to "burn and rave at close of day," to "rage against the dying of the light"?[19] I have tried to anticipate my death in meditation and to an extent have envisioned myself in the box with mourners around, but that is really not me in the box. It is some idealized or projected me, and it is still not even then a dead me. How can one anticipate his own non-existence? It's impossible.

The only way I can meet my death is by acknowledging that it will come, and that it already has in the limitations that entomb me. To accept limitations and yet to see them as not limiting is perhaps to experience death and yet to discover within death that life is present. Perhaps Eliot was right in saying: "I have seen birth and death but had thought they were different."[20] Maybe they really aren't. Perhaps they are only two faces of a single event, and that death is that event viewed from the point of view of its limitations, that birth is viewed from the point of view of its possibilities—or is it that I just need to make tombs into wombs?

Chapter 14
John 13:1—13:31
From Served to Servant

With the advent of chapter 13 John comes to a new turning point in his gospel. We will witness now a new focus of energy, a different intensity of teaching, less polemic against his adversaries, and a new depth of intimacy with his disciples. There are three broad areas for consideration: (1) the meal and its surrounding "happenings" (chapters 13 to 17), (2) the passion and death (chapters 18 to 19), and (3) the resurrection stories (chapters 20 to 21).

Different commentators on these chapters tend to capture different aspects of the change I refer to in the way in which they emphasize what is happening. Thus Schnackenburg talks about Jesus in "the circle of his own,"[1] drawing our attention to the intimacy between them. Brown refers to this whole section as "The Book of Glory" because it focuses on the "hour" of Jesus, on his passion, death, resurrection and ascension, as the moment in which he is glorified.[2] Crossan draws our attention to the change in language in these chapters. John, who up until now often used the words life, to live, to give life (fifty times) and light, barely uses them at all in the remaining chapters. He will use life six times and light not at all. On the other hand the word "love," which appeared only six times in the first half of the gospel, now appears thirty-one times. Crossan concludes that the change in "terms" makes it clear that "to abide in love is to have life and light together to exist fully, and to know how and why we do so."[3]

The first major segment of this half of the gospel is the meal (chapters 13 to 14). In itself this has three large segments:

(a) the meal (chapter 13);
(b) the discourse at the meal (chapters 14 to 16);
(c) the prayer of Jesus (chapter 14).

Each needs to be approached separately. The meal section is first, and it too can be seen to have three sections worth attention: (a) the meal; (b) Judas; (c) the disciples. It is to this section therefore that we now turn our attention.

Perhaps the first question we need to ask is: What kind of meal is this that Jesus is having with the disciples? In the synoptic gospels, or at least in Luke and Matthew, it appears to be a Passover meal and Jesus is clearly shown getting ready for it. He desires it, he organizes it, he gives the disciples specific instructions on how to procure the room, where it is to be celebrated, etc. In John's gospel, however, it is apparently not a Passover meal that is being shared since John specifically mentions that it was on the night before the Passover that they got together. Nor does it appear to have been a Eucharistic meal since John does not use the "words of institution" as we see in the synoptics.

What kind of meal is this, then, at which they gather?

It certainly was not a joyful meal, at least when looked at from one point of view. The events leading to it indicate a great deal of strain and tension. Jesus has been speaking pretty consistently about his "hour," and even if the disciples have not clearly grasped what this involves, Jesus certainly sees it as an hour which is marked by death. During the meal there is a pretty high level of tension reflected in his announcement that there is a betrayer in the group, and in the questions that they address to him.

Not only is this happening within the meal, but all around this group other events are taking shape which cannot but affect them and their evening together. The tension and hostility of the Jews is growing. Their plotting is becoming more apparent and their intentions more evident. They have given an order that "if anyone knows where he [Jesus] was they should report it so that they might seize him" (13:1). The meal clearly is affected by these tensions.

What kind of meal is it, then, that they celebrate? It is a last supper, a farewell meal, a leave-taking meal. It is goodbye time, and Jesus has called them together because he is obviously, as the discourse section shows, concerned with the impact that his departure will have on the disciples. There is here another touch of John's irony: the farewell discourse, which takes up nearly a fifth of the whole gospel, is now placed in the mouth of Jesus the life-giver.

A related question needs to be asked. Who was at this meal? Who were the disciples he was addressing during the evening? Was it only the "twelve" or was it a larger and more inclusive group? Were there men and women in the group? Schüssler Fiorenza maintains that the Johannine Jesus has his last supper "not just with the twelve but with all the disciples, and that the fourth gospel never stresses the leadership of the twelve among the disciples, for all the members of the community have received the Spirit. The

Johannine community of friends understands itself primarily as a community of disciples."[4] If this is so it obviously has great import for the course of "women's issues" in the church and for the future direction of its theology.

Rather than pursuing the theological implications of this we will return to the meal. Jesus is reported by John to wash the feet of the disciples who were there, whoever they were. The foot washing is relayed to us in such a way that it cannot be perceived as a mere accident or a peripheral part of the evening. John is the only one of the evangelists to record it. It has special significance for him. In fact he sets the tone for it deliberately by telling us that it was a moment of full consciousness for Jesus. He was at this moment conscious of his origin and his end, of where he came from and where he was going, and in that situation John shows him acting very deliberately. Six verbs attest to it. John says, "He rose from the table, took off his outward garment, tied a towel around his waist, poured water into a basin, and began to wash his disciples' feet and dry them with a towel."

What is the significance and meaning of this very conscious and deliberate action? There are some precedents in the culture to help us understand, but here they prove inadequate. It was common in ancient Palestine to wash the feet of guests in one's home as an act of courtesy. This was especially true if they had journeyed a long way in the desert, etc. This washing, however, was done at the moment of entry to the house, not at the end of the meal. We must look elsewhere for our understanding, since here Jesus performs his act at the end of the meal. The customary washing that I refer to was normally performed by a non-Jewish slave, but on occasion a group of disciples might do it for their rabbi as a special sign of respect. It was never done by the rabbi for the student. Here it is the rabbi who acts as the slave-servant for the disciples, and he does so with full awareness of what he is doing in placing himself in that position.

John himself provides us with two interpretations of the foot washing. In verses 6 to 10 the explanation comes in response to Peter's misunderstanding of the event and his subsequent refusal to have Jesus wash his feet. Jesus tells Peter that without the washing he cannot participate in the inheritance—he will not share eternal life. The foot washing in this context symbolizes Jesus' death, the ultimate act of humility. A second explanation is given a little later on in verses 12 to 17. Here Jesus tells them he has given them an example. He acts as a model for them so that in his posture and life style they can perceive how they must be from now on if they are to be his disciples. In both explanations John draws attention to Judas. He notes how "all but one are clean" in the first explanation, and in the second he says, "I am not talking about all of you. . . . The man who ate my bread has turned against me."

While there are two explanations of the foot washing, and they are related, I intend to focus on the second. I see Jesus here teaching the disciples how they are to be church in the future. They are to do what he does and has been doing. When we glance back through the gospel we see that he has always been showing them how to go from the periphery to the center, from the outside to the inside, from being ministered to by others to being the ones who now do the ministering, from being the recipient to being the servant, from being the spectator to being the participant. Here now I see him in this action drawing attention to the shape of ministry and to the meaning of life which it reflects. As I become aware of that, my thoughts flash back to the other incidents in the gospel in which he was dealing with this topic, and I see him teaching these things to them:

1. in the story of the early chapters where he was showing them that mission was foundational to ministry and that the other side of being called is to discover that at the same time we are sent out to the world.
2. in the Nicodemus story when he stresses that ministry involves a movement from secrecy to openness, from doubt of self to trust of self.
3. in the dialogue of the Samaritan woman when he shows that while self-centeredness and egocentricity may be our starting point, we must go beyond that to telling others what God has done for us. Ministry is witnessing to others, witness in the context of a community.
4. in the story of the paralyzed man where ministry is reflected as a non-willingness to victimize the victim for one's condition and being willing to ask the other to delineate one's need. This involves converting our own loneliness into a creative solitude as well as a way of imaging and imagining a world.
5. in the story of the feeding where ministry involves very concrete needs as well as physical and spiritual ones. Ministry here involves a movement from responsibility to a willingness to respond to self and others. It involves personal spontaneity to the exigencies of a situation that in turn stimulates response in others.
6. in the story of Tabernacles where ministry is shown to be a choice and that it cannot be imposed. It involves a movement from unfreedom to freedom, from slavery to the things that bind to openness in a prayerful and liturgical context to the things that call us to freedom and wholeness.
7. in the story of the woman taken in adultery where ministry is reflected in the tension between challenge and acceptance, in the ability to be the reconciling one

because one has been reconciled and also in a willingness to grow and develop psychosexually.

8. in the story of the blind man where Jesus shows ministry as a willingness to see the real, to see what is
because one is no longer under the sway of illusions and
old ways of looking at things.

9. in the story of the sheep and the shepherd where ministry is perceived as knowledge of the person more than
knowledge about the person.

10. in the Lazarus story where ministry involves death and
life, a willingness to accept the consequences of one's
action, where ministry is perceived as entering structures of death as a life summoning agent even though
one knows what the fall out of that will be.

The above are just some of the gospel's hints at what
is involved in ministry. Some of them reflect some of what
we saw in the other chapters but obviously have more to
teach us when examined more fully from this perspective.
It seems to me that the foot washing points backward to all
those moments, as it also points forward to the death that
is coming. Without the two-edged sword there is no
inheritance.

It is important, however, when we consider this example of Jesus that we keep in mind that what Jesus is doing
here is not playing a part. This is not a performance from
which he can slip aside at the end of the meal. He does not
play the role of servant here and then subsequently withdraw from it. Here being a servant expresses who he is. His
existence and vocation are identical. The act reflects the
reality of who he is even as who he is demands the action
that is his life.

By contrast the second scene (verses 18 to 30) reflects
someone who is at the other pole, whose life is all a role.

Judas appears to go through all the motions. He heard the call, came to Jesus, went with him on mission, partook of the meal, etc., but at the meal it becomes apparent that he has been playing a role. There is no substance. Jesus even affords him the opportunity to withdraw from the role, to integrate his role and his life, to become part of the reality, to accept life with Jesus, but even here Judas cannot. He accepts the bread that is offered, but neither the friendship nor the hospitality that goes with it. He cannot accept the invitation and symbolically withdraws from the community, enters isolation, and goes out into what John clearly calls "the night."

Judas is presented to us in the gospel as one who never quite got his act together. Already in 6:70 Jesus says, "One of you is a devil," and we are told that he was "talking of Judas, the son of Simon Iscariot." Now at the start of the farewell meal he tells us that "the devil had already decided that Judas the son of Simon Iscariot would betray Jesus" (13:2). Again a little later on he says that "as soon as Judas took the bread Satan went into him" (13:27). Judas, there-fore, says Culpepper, "is related to the children of the devil who hate and kill, in much the same way as the beloved disciple is related to the children of God who are marked by love."[5] If it is Jesus and the Father who enter into the disciples' hearts and take up residence there, it is Satan who enters the heart of Judas. He is therefore for Culpepper the "representative defector."[6]

When Judas goes out into the night he has in reality refused any self-knowledge, which had been offered to him, and which could have been his in the accepting of the bread. From that point on there is a different flow of energy perceived in the way the respective "ministries" of Judas and Jesus evolve. There is a sense of immediacy and impa-tience about Judas that leads him to participate in violence to get it over with. There is a sense of closure and calm about Jesus which allows him to say farewell. There is a sense in which Judas now awaits the world as its lord, hoping and expecting it to serve his needs, while Jesus moves out as servant to the need of the world. Judas tries to find security which will keep him from death; Jesus moves out to embrace it. Judas joins forces with violence for money; Jesus joins forces with peace for community. Judas is washed by Jesus at the supper but in the end he remains "not clean"; he remains in the darkness of night, lost in a futile attempt to make the world and its people serve his own egocentric hungers.

I come to the first scene of the last supper now in prayer and it brings me home to my own life and its attendant struggles. I watch Jesus giving this example in the circle of his own, and I find myself wondering what that looks like in my own life. I recognize that the tradition of the church has incarnated ways of living out this example of Jesus in what it has called the spiritual and corporal works of mercy. The corporal works flow out of Matthew 25 and they are: to feed the hungry, give drink to the thirsty, clothe the naked, visit the sick, attend to those in prison, give shelter to the homeless and bury the dead. The spiritual works are also seven in number and are traditionally listed as follows: to admonish the sinner, instruct the ignorant, counsel the doubtful, comfort the sorrowful, bear wrongs patiently, forgive all injuries and pray for the living and the dead. Even as I look at them I find myself wondering: What is the service to which my life is given? How is it a ministry? In what ways am I invited deeper into the ministry by the core of my life? To what, if anything, am I committed? It is not just a question of what I might be willing to die for, but the much more difficult question of what am I willing to live for in the future. Put another way, I might ask: What is it that my life up to now has testified to, and is that what I want it to continue to say? Am I in service only to my own ego-centric desires or to something larger? Whose need is my life meeting? My own? Others'? The world's? Am I in fact coming in contact with the mystery that I am in the midst of the facts that form my existence?

I watch Jesus with these questions in me, and as I do it seems to me that what occasioned his sadness was the discovery of his own ultimate ineffectiveness, his inability to get others to accept the love he offered them. John makes it clear throughout the gospel that some people preferred the darkness to the light and that in the end Judas was deciding to go out into the night. Jesus' loving him as he did permitted him to do this even though he wished better for him. I wonder if this is the way it is between me and my self. Is my ministry a choosing of the darkness or the light? Is it a refusal or acceptance of the self? Are my life and my vocation becoming one or are they separating into roles that do not know each other?

I watch Jesus again, and this time I am drawn to his fidelity, and it leads me to think about fidelity in my own life. To what? To whom? Fidelity to the ego can be infidelity to the self. It can, I begin to see, be an acceptance of the bread without the acceptance of either the hospitality or the wholeness that go with it. Is service to the self selfishness or self-centeredness, positive or negative, darkness or light? Anthony Padovano notes that there "is an essential difference between a specific vocation which one lives so that he may love others and the comfort of a self-advantageous situation which one hypocritically uses as a vocation. In the latter case one does not encounter fidelity but deception, even self-deception."[7] I look, I wonder, and I ask whose feet I wash.

I find myself in my meditation reflecting that I am and

that the self that I am is a gift. The way I accept it or reject it is an example of the service I render others. I sit, I watch, I listen, and the question of Jesus comes to lodge in my heart: "Do you know what I have done for you?" and out of all the confusion that simple question engenders, I resolve to not abandon myself but to be who and what I am as I am in this moment that I am.

Chapter 15
John 13:31—16:31
From Me to You

Following the foot washing there now comes a time for talking, as indeed occurs at most banquet affairs. Jesus wants to talk about his separation from those he loves and cares for and with whom he has eaten. In fact there are two separations going on here. One is final and the other is temporary. The first separation is from the world. This is final and it is referred to as judgment. The world, the unbelievers, will not see him again, and so his farewell to them is final. It is also their death (8:21ff). The second separation is from the disciples. It has more of the flavor of "until we meet again" about it. He tells them that for a little while they will see him, then for a little while they will not see him, and then a little while again and they will see him. This separation, therefore, I call temporary, and it is this separation that we will concern ourselves with in this chapter instead of the former.

The farewell speech or discourse itself embraces chapters 14 through 16. It is a lengthy speech and probably was not delivered at one time.[1] It is more of a composite than anything else. It concerns three important phases which to my way of thinking all lead to the same place. Jesus is concerned to deal with three elements:

1. the questions that are on the minds and in the hearts of the disciples;
2. the emotional state and anxiety that they are experiencing at the thought of his coming departure;
3. the need to provide for their future time together in a world where they will experience hatred, etc.

There are four questions phrased during the course of the supper discussion. These questions can be looked at from different points of view, but the thing they have in common that catches my attention is that they all in one way or another reflect some kind of misunderstanding of Christ. This forms part of a pattern of misunderstandings in the gospel as a whole, and as such they are worthy of our attention.[2] Let us turn therefore to each of the questions in turn.

The first question is asked by Peter who says to Jesus, "Where do you mean to go?" When Jesus tells him, "I am going where you cannot follow me now; later on you shall come after me," Peter shows by his response a great willingness to be with Jesus but a rather poor understanding of what is happening. Peter—and John cleverly has him borrow words from the Good Shepherd story—says, "I will lay down my life for you." His answer implies a knowledge of Jesus, a mutual understanding (I know mine and mine know me), as well as an intention. The truth, however, is that Peter doesn't really know why he can't follow. He doesn't know that it really will cost him his life. Peter is all desire and resolve, but it springs from a state of total inflation. Soon that tire will break. Peter will deny Christ three times, and in the ensuing deflation he will begin to realize why he cannot "now" follow. For the moment his question merely reflects a misunderstanding of why Jesus had to die.

Thomas is the second questioner. His question in some ways reveals him to be a mirror image of Peter. He says: "Lord, we do not know where you are going; how can we know the way to get there?" He is at the other end of the spectrum. In some ways, as the *Jerome Biblical Commentary*[3] suggests, he reflects the ignorance of all the disciples. He is a realist, a practical man, at home in the world of the flesh. He understands Jesus in the flesh but he doesn't understand the glory. He cannot understand how Jesus' death is his exaltation. The logic does not compute. It does not fit into the practicalities of life. His question then reflects his misunderstanding of what is happening in the death of Jesus.

Philip follows next in line. We have previously mentioned how in chapter 1, when the other disciples were called to see, Philip was called to follow. Then we said that a crisis would come for Philip. This is it. He cannot see, he cannot share the vision. He asks Jesus to show him the Father. His question too reflects a misunderstanding. Grady relates his difficulty to that of Martin Buber. He says, "Evidently he is bothered by the very objection Buber raises regarding Christ; Israel believes in the one God who cannot be represented or confined to any outward form, but in Christ the presence of the one who cannot be represented, the paradox of Emunah, is replaced by the binatarian image of God, one aspect of which, turned towards the man, shows him a human face."[4] Apparently Philip is still awaiting some great new sign. He does not appear to have grasped at all that Jesus and the Father are one. He too misunderstands and expresses his confusion about what Jesus is saying in this question that he asks at the farewell meal.

Judas is the fourth questioner. This, John is careful to point out, is not Judas Iscariot the betrayer, but the other Judas. He is probably Judas the son of James whom Luke (6:16) tells us about and names as one of the apostles. He too has a significant question to ask which will also reveal that he is among those who misunderstands. He asks, "Lord, why is it that you will reveal yourself to us and not to the world?" Why, he wonders, does Jesus reveal himself to some and not to all? The question recalls another incident in the gospel when in 7:3 the disciples suggested to Jesus that it was time to display his miracles to the world. It reflects a misunderstanding about how Jesus will reveal himself. He still thinks—and he is like Philip in this—that Jesus is going to pull off the upset of the year with some great show of power, etc. He has not yet grasped that the revelation Jesus gives is by and through his indwelling. He misunderstands the method of Jesus' revelation.

These incidents of misunderstanding at the last supper on the part of the disciples are not isolated moments.[5] They form part of the pattern that characterizes the disciples throughout the gospel. We have seen them misunderstand Jesus when he spoke to them about the temple of his body (2:21), and when he told them during the course of his conversation with the Samaritan woman that he had food that they knew nothing at all about (4:32). During the course of the conversation about Lazarus' death they also misunderstood him when he said that he was only asleep and that he would go and wake him up (11:11-15), and finally they misunderstood him at the moment of the entry into Jerusalem (12:16).

This pattern of misunderstandings reveals the character of the disciples as it evolves in the gospel. Segovia in particular points to four distinct stages through which the disciples are characterized in the gospel, and he delineates them as follows:

1. There is the gathering of the elect by Jesus and the initial confrontation of the world (chapters 1–3).
2. The elect on their way with Jesus and the growing rejection of the world (chapters 4–12).
3. The farewell to the elect by Jesus and the exclusion of the world (chapters 13–14).
4. The vindication of the elect and the judgment of the world (chapters 18–20).[6]

Segovia maintains that in the first two stages a contrast is shown between the disciples and the Jews of Jerusalem. The disciples follow while the Jews oppose him. The disciples do not understand him, but, says Segovia, John counterbalances this by giving futher action or teaching on Jesus' part. In the third section, which is what we are considering here, John shows us, says Segovia, the real reason for the disciples' failure to understand. It is because the Spirit has not yet been given. It is only when this happens in the fourth stage of the gospel that the theme of the disciples' incomprehension is reversed; finally the disciples do see the meaning and significance of the hour and do perceive Jesus' full status as God's unique representative.[7]

Not only does Jesus respond to the disciples' questions but he also responds to their emotional situation. This becomes clear more from looking at his responses than from anything that is said directly about them. There are, I believe, at least five passages that are helpful here. He tells them:

(a) not to be worried and upset. He will prepare a place for them and he will come back to take them with him (14:3).
(b) that he will not leave them alone, that he will not leave them orphans, that he will not abandon them but rather that he will come back to them (14:18).

(c) that he knows they will be in the world, that there they will encounter hatred, but they are to remember that if the world hates them, the reason is because they do not belong to it. He has chosen them out of the world (15:18).

(d) that his going away is indeed painful but that it will be followed by joy. It is therefore, he says, more like the pangs of birth that they are going to go through, and then he will come back to them and nobody will take away the ensuing joy and all their questions will be quieted and stilled (16:21–22).

(e) that during the time he is away he leaves them his peace. This peace, however, is not peace in the way the world gives peace (15:27 and 16:33).

These passages then reflect the condition of the disciples and also Jesus' move to meet that very real grieving that they were already beginning. He knows that they will be broken and indeed shattered on many different levels, and he moves to surface it to consciousness where he and they can begin to cope with it together. He keeps accepting their feelings and injecting a hope into the abyss of pain that his departure elevates. He indicates that following his separation there will be a newness; a new era, a new association will form, an era of the Spirit. His farewell discourse then is an attempt, not wholly successful if their questions are any indication, to meet their rising negative emotions. It attempts to transform the negative into the positive by pointing to the fact that pain will turn to joy, absence to presence, isolation to community, death into birth, and fear into courage. This happens, he says, when the Spirit comes to abide with them.

It is finally therefore to the Spirit that Jesus now turns in the farewell discourse. What he says here, however, does not stand apart from what he has said elsewhere in the gospel. John constantly refers to the Spirit as "he," and I will follow that in my remarks. It is obvious, however, that we cannot in this short space attempt to cover the whole teaching on the Spirit in John's gospel, and so we shall indicate more a direction than anything else. It is true that, as Painter suggests, "John more than any other writer in the New Testament presents us with the evidence which forced the early church almost against its will to formulate the doctrine of the Trinity."[8] Here, however, in the farewell discourse, it is a "functional" view of the Spirit that we are given, and it is presented to us in five passages (14:16;14:26;15:26;16:7–11;16:13). We are not then dealing with the gifts of the Spirit as Paul delineates them, nor are we dealing with the "processions" of the Trinity as theology is concerned with in its deliberations. We are concerned with the Spirit himself.

The first thing we notice is the promise that the Spirit will come. The word he uses is "Paraclete," which is an interesting choice of words since it can be translated in different ways. Two ways of translating it come from the legal system.[9] Perhaps there is a play on words involved since, as De La Potterie reminds us, "the whole life of Jesus is presented in the fourth gospel within the juridical framework of what is called the great trial."[10] The word "Paraclete" can be translated through this legal system as meaning either Advocate, that is, one who speaks on behalf of a client, or Intercessor, which is more one who pleads for the client to the judge after the verdict. Two other words are used to translate the term "Paraclete." The word "Comforter" involves the idea of a consoling presence, while the word "Proclaimer" reflects more the idea of exhortation and uplifting. The word therefore is open to subtleties in translation with slightly different connotations.

It is interesting to note that Jesus tells the apostles he will send them "another" Paraclete because this implies that they already had received a previous one. Who is that? Brown[11] makes the observation that "everything that is said of the Spirit in these passages has already been said of Jesus in the gospel," thus leading us to understand that Jesus himself was the first Paraclete. Thus both Jesus and the Paraclete are sent by the Father, recognized by believers, teachers who lead believers into truth, bear witness to Jesus, and convict the world of sin. Nevertheless there is a difference. The Paraclete is not Jesus, no more than Jesus is the Father. The Paraclete is dependent upon the Father and the Son and will not come if the Son does not go.

What is the function of the Paraclete in these passages? He is primarily the teacher. Jesus tells them that the Paraclete will speak only what he hears, that he will not speak on his own authority and that he will lead them into all truth. This may look a little confusing if we forget that for John truth is not a Hellenistic concept. He gets his idea of truth from the "apocalyptic and wisdom literature"[12] of the Old Testament, says De La Potterie, and on the basis of that he maintains that for John truth is a person. The Spirit's action is completely Christ-centered. His function is to teach and lead them deeper into a relationship with the truth that is the revelation of God, with the truth that is the revealed word of God, with the truth that is Christ. The new era then, the second phase of revelation, the function of the Spirit, will not be to bring a new revelation but to display in clear light the word of revelation, of Jesus. The function of the Spirit might be said then to awaken people, or, better still, to make people conscious, to bring to their awareness something or rather someone they have up to now only half understood.

Jesus says to the apostles that the Spirit will witness

and that they too will witness. What is the difference between the two? De La Potterie points to it when he says that the "Spirit will be an inner witness in their hearts so that they in turn may be able to witness before men."[13] The Spirit's witness is a question of a completely interior action; it consists in bringing them to a knowledge of the truth. The community will also witness. It will proclaim Jesus by its life of brotherly love, but the Spirit will give the power and interior energy to fulfill the love life.

I come home to this farewell address of Jesus, to this absence that will be a deeper realization of his presence, and as I do I am struck by the care and loving concern of Jesus. I believe that at the center of my self there is this openness to God and to humanity. I also believe that from it there flows what can best be called an energy, a breath, a life-giving force that will not act contrary to the deepest desires of my heart if it is permitted to act. I believe that this energizing force, this essentially life-giving, formative dynamic movement, will lead me out of myself, will lead me beyond the limits, and that it is in going there that I will discover the deeper revelation of who I am. It is in the going out that I can therefore remain within, and it is in the remaining within that I am ever able to move out. The external manifestation of that is the love I bear the men and women who enter my life and whose lives I enter; the interior dimension of it is the Spirit, ever ancient, ever new. Because I shrink from the going out I diminish the within, because I can remain periodically within, I have hope ultimately not for separation from all that is but for a relationship, which is to say I have "hope" for a Spirit-filled life because of the gift of the Spirit, which is relational.

Chapter 16
John 17:1—17:24
From Son to Father

In John 17 Jesus addresses a solemn prayer to his Father in the presence of his disciples. Commonly referred to as the high priestly prayer because of its intercessory quality, it is perhaps more appropriately titled the shepherd's prayer by Schillebeeckx[1] since here Jesus is giving his life for his flock. Whether the prayer was in fact spoken at the last supper meal or not, or whether it was spoken in its current form or not, is a question that scholars have not completed debating. It is, however, a very intense, intimate and indeed climactic moment in Jesus' life in the form in which it is presented to us. In and through this prayer we are therefore allowed to enter upon the heart of Christ.

The prayer takes much of its intensity from the situation in which it appears. At the moment of death people frequently speak of the things that have concerned them most in life. Elisabeth Kübler Ross and others clearly testify to that fact.[2] People at these moments come back to basics, to the things that have made life most meaningful and important for them. Jesus is no exception. It is clear to him now that death is imminent. He has seen and felt the growing hostility. He has watched the plans begin to develop. Perhaps the betrayal by Judas has taken place. All these are pointers to him that death is coming and that therefore the time of parting from the apostles is close at hand. His prayer then is a prayer addressed to the Father at the time of his departure. In fact Brown compares it favorably with the canticle of Moses at the time of his departure from the people as it is given in Deuteronomy 32.[3]

The prayer gives evidence, as is true of all Jesus says and does, in John, of the relationship existing between the Father and himself. It does not stand apart from all that has been building between them in the gospel. Rather it intensifies it. It is therefore the outgrowth and climax of an intense relationship between them. John has already said in 5:19 that the Son does what the Father does. In 5:26 we see that as the Father has life in himself, so he has granted to the Son to have life in himself. Later on the great fidelity of both to the relationship is attested to when Jesus says: "The one who sent me is with me now. He has not deserted me since I always do what pleases him"; and in 10:30 we are told: "My Father and I are one." It is to this relationship, which seems to dominate the mind of Jesus, that he returns again at the last supper when he says to the disciples, "Believe me, that I am in the Father, and the Father is in me." This relationship is the context that occasions his prayer as it has done frequently in the gospel, or, as Schnackenburg puts it, Jesus prayed in the gospel but "it is never a petition based on human need. . . . Because he is one with God he prays, and because he prays he is one with God."[4]

The prayer that comes to his lips now at the moment of departure reflects an ever widening circle of care that spreads outward from that relationship. The prayer has three phases. (a) It begins with Jesus praying for himself. (b) It develops to embrace the disciples. (c) Finally it enlarges to take in the wider community who will come to believe because of their words. In each of these circles there is a key word which, it seems to me, reflects the concerns of Jesus. The first is "glory"; then, as his thought moves to the apostles, the word "world" seems to gain an ascendancy; finally, when he thinks of the wider community, the word "unity" comes to the forefront. It is therefore to these three segments of the prayer that we now turn our attention.

From the beginning of the gospel John has stressed the "glory of God." He has insisted very strongly that the reality of God is available, accessible and visible in Jesus. People can approach the reality of God through him. In the prologue he states: "We have seen his glory, the glory as of the only Son of the Father." There is throughout the gospel a gradual and progressive revelation from the moment of the incarnation that manifests God's glory. All the signs, all the works that Jesus does, reveal something of this glory. In a sense this movement is the very opposite to that of Paul where Jesus is continually emptying himself and humbling himself until the moment of the cross.[5] Then death becomes the ultimate humility. For John death and the cross are the "hour" of glory. The movement is like a movement upward to the cross, while Paul's is by contrast a movement downward. The two movements are, of course, one, looked at from two different sides. Death is for John the moment of exaltation and glorification. Therefore, he will not pray to avoid it. He prays for its coming.

The glory of God is the outward manifestation of God's own life and excellence. It stands in contrast to another phrase we find in the gospel called the "glory of man."

Many, we are told, loved the glory of men rather than the glory of God. In fact, in three places in the gospel Jesus finds this second kind of concern a real obstacle to faith. In 5:41–44 this kind of glory is presented as honor, praise or approval given by men. Christ will say to them: "You like to have praise from one another but you do not try to win praise from God." In 7:18 and 8:50 he describes such a person as interested in self-advancement and self-exaltation. "A person who speaks on his own is trying to gain glory for himself" (17:18). It is love then for a greatness and pre-eminence apart from God, and it prevents acceptance of Christ. Christ, however, shows the Father's glory, seeks the Father's glory, and reveals the Father's glory, and he does this by showing forth himself, by revealing who he is to people, the Son of God made man. The Father also glorifies this Son. It is a two-way street. In each step of the gospel not only is Jesus showing who God is but God is showing forth who Jesus is, his only Son full of grace and truth. In praying now for "glory" Jesus is not asking or petitioning for anything for himself. He is not seeking approval of people, power, etc. He is interested rather in the recognition of the Father and also, as we shall see, in the welfare of his disciples.

In the second part of the prayer the care for the disciples emerges as he prays for them. His prayer is that they may be dedicated to the truth and kept safe from the evil one. He asks therefore not that they be taken out of the world but that they be protected. John's use of the word "world" is not consistent in the gospel. Sometimes he uses it in a rather "natural" way, and when he does he seems to be referring to the physical world itself (cf. 17:24). Sometimes he uses the word but qualifies it with another word, "this," which suggests the existence of another world. In fact we find such an expression on ten occasions in the gospel. There is therefore for John a heavenly world as opposed to an earthly world, a world above as distinct from a world below. On other occasions we find a third usage of the word "world," as when he speaks of the world as created by the Logos, the world loved by God. John's "world" therefore is a rather complex one. It is a "world of tensions with a wide range of implications which are barely compatible with one another, extending from an almost completely natural concept of the world to one which signifies mankind's persistent and rigid unbelief."[6]

John's attitude to the world is best understood against the background of the expulsion of the Christians from the synagogue.[7] This factor had a great influence on the formation of the gospel, and Neyrey suggests that it had four discernible effects upon the Christological confession in the gospel. These he describes as follows: (1) it confirms the fact that Jesus was not of this world; (2) it describes Jesus as other-worldly and maintains that this is to be acknowledged and confessed; (3) there is in consequence a corresponding devaluation of this world; (4) the confession of Jesus as a heavenly figure becomes what Neyrey calls the "touchstone of authentic membership."[8] This brief explanation can help us put into some focus the passage we are now dealing with in chapter 17. Here the world seems to have a somewhat negative character. It is a place from which hatred and hostility emerge. Jesus, however, does not seem overly concerned with this; he doesn't seem to try to prevent it from happening. He recognizes that the disciples must live in the midst of this, and so he sends them into the world but prays that they be kept safe, that they be protected. There is, then, a recognition of the dangers that they must endure and that there is the possibility that they may be lost. During the Gethsemani scene (18:5–8) as we shall see the soldiers will come to arrest Jesus, and then

Jesus will use the divine name "ego eimi" not only as a statement of identity but as a statement which both protects the apostles and renders the soldiers harmless and powerless. Here we have a somewhat similar situation. Jesus prays for the apostles and asks the Father to "consecrate" them in the truth. John Sheets[9] has noted that the whole of Christ's presence in the gospel of John is a "consecrating presence," and we have seen throughout the gospel how Jesus himself is consecrated becoming the new temple and how through him all the feasts, institutions, and people of the Old Testament are consecrated and given new meaning. There are, says Sheets, "in addition new rites of consecration, baptism and the Eucharist" to take the place of the old rites.[10] Jesus' prayer then is that the disciples now be consecrated so that they will come into recognition of the truth. When this happens they will come into the recognition of their own being, their own identity, their own life, and they will recognize that the life they share with him is the same life he shares with the Father.

In the third segment of this prayer the circle widens. Jesus' horizon shifts again to embrace not only the disciples but also all those who will believe because of their words. This part of his prayer has three segments to it. He prays that the disciples will be united like the Father and the Son, that they will be united in the Father and the Son, and that they will manifest the unity of the Father and the Son by the love that they have within and among themselves which will characterize their behavior. Their love is to be not only a love of service and sacrifice, but it must go beyond that to a love of union. Jesus asks the Father that they be an example in both energy and relationship so that what goes on, and what happens between them, will reflect the "glory" of God. The model of unity that he prays they will achieve is that which exists between the Father and

Son; it is that which exists in the Trinity, which, as Brown points out, is "not just a moral unity but a vital organic unity in which the Father gives life to the Son."[11]

I find it helpful in pursuing these thoughts to turn to Teilhard de Chardin who expresses his belief that there are two possible forms of conceiving ultimate unity, two different ways in which humankind searches for the Absolute. He called these by different names but most commonly spoke of two roads, that of the East and of the West.[12] These two roads have been associated with the religions of the East and of the West, respectively. They express two types or approaches to union. What he calls the road of the East is characterized by an attempt to escape from matter, from the world, from the earth, from a confusing and unsettling multiplicity. It promotes a sense of withdrawal from things and of detachment. It stresses the power of prayer as contemplation which will eventually lead to a person's identification with the absolute, with the all, with God. It leads in Teilhard's view to a dissolution of personality rather than to its perfection. By contrast there is what he calls the road of the West which also brings about union, but it is a union by differentiation. Here the one in a sense emerges from the multiple. Union is effected over time. There is a gradual transformation and convergence of multiple elements into a higher center. Matter, the world, the earth, etc., are transformed through energy, through action. Union with God does not involve the passivity of the person but rather an active convergence and concentration. For Teilhard ultimate unity may be found either at the base through the elimination of opposites between things or at the apex through ultra-differentiation. One type of union is that of salt with sea where the salt loses its own identity and becomes the sea. The other is that of differentiation. True union does not fuse the elements it brings together; by mutual fertilization and adaptation it gives them a renewal of vitality. It is egoism, says Teilhard, that hardens and neutralizes the human stuff. Union differentiates. He sees that humankind today has reached a critical point. It is at a crossroad wondering which way to go. Will it take the road East or the road West, or will there be a convergence of roads, and the formation and development, the emergence of a new mysticism which he calls the mysticism of unification and of love. This new mysticism would be cosmic mysticism in which God is loved not above all things but in and through all things.

We seem to have wandered a little in our meditation on this chapter of John, and yet the wandering has been purposive. As we return now we can begin to draw together some of the key thoughts in the chapter and see them in terms of a story of self. Obviously death, the separation, the breaking up of the relationship with the apostles, is what triggers Jesus' prayer. Here he expresses his concern for them that in their relationship they may be a true unity and that they may be protected from the world, from falling into its grasp, and that this unity (by differentiation) may reflect who God is, manifest God's glory. This is the challenge he issues to them; it is a somewhat similar challenge that we go through as we grow as persons. We are initially born into a world where the psyche operates with a sense of undifferentiated wholeness. We exist in what Neumann calls a field of "unitary reality."[13] Growth then is growth into consciousness as the self begins to manifest in the ego, or as the ego comes to birth out of the unconscious. Growing involves initially the establishment and strengthening of the ego to the apparent loss of the self. The ego adapts to the external world through the development of what Jung[14] calls its superior functions and the repression of what Jung calls the inferior functions. As life continues to unfold, however, all the functions must be claimed, all must be allowed to exist. Gradually we come to the realization that much of us exists outside ourselves where we have projected it. Growth therefore involves now the reclaiming of these parts of ourselves which we have unconsciously given to the other. It involves therefore the meeting with what Jung calls the shadow, the animus, the anima. Only in this way can we free ourselves to be us and free others to be themselves. Only in this way, then, is relationship possible. Only in this way do we prepare ourselves to discover where we are going, what we are moving toward, what our teleological significance is; only in this way can we reach the radically other that is God. This discovery delimits the ego and relativizes it. The self that I am and that I am becoming proclaims the mystery that remains. Unity by differentiation, I am not the other, my thoughts are not my feelings, unity by cooperation, relatedness, and charity (the other has much to exchange with me person to person, feeling to thought, etc.), and glorification through unification (the manifestation of the self within and contact and proclamation of the God without) follow. The prayer of Christ becomes the living prayer of Christians.

Reflecting therefore on this chapter as a story of self leads me to the realization again that the self is the life-bearer. The self is God's gift poured out for man, and we are called to believe in it and to listen to it and its revelatory message. Three elements, however, can frustrate this, which have been traditionally called the flesh, the world and the devil, or which we can call in the light of this chapter human glory, this world, and multiplicity or plurality. These three are part of the reality into which we were birthed. They are part of the fabric of life and constitutive of human existence. In a sense Mark's gospel emphasizes their activity and gives us an understanding of how they work: their name is legion, they multiply, their last state is worse than the first, etc. In John the emphasis by contrast is on Jesus' activity. In John we see the antidote. In Mark there is a battle leading to crucifixion; in John there is transcendence by crucifixion. What we see in Mark is Jesus naming the evil powers, battling with them, and conquering them. What we see in John is Jesus attending to the Father and entering into a deeper relationship with him. The consciousness that the self has that the ego does not is not just that God exists but that God loves, and this assurance and awareness can transform the wounds of living. It transcends suffering, uniting by differentiating and glorifying by revealing.

Chapter 17
John 18:1—19:42
From Humiliation to Exaltation

I think there are special moments in everybody's life that seem to have a focusing effect. Everything that goes before that moment seems somehow to have been a preparation for it, and everything that follows it seems to take meaning from it. For some it's winning an Olympic medal, for others it may be a war, for others it may be marriage, etc. Such a moment in John's gospel is the passion. Everything that Jesus did brought him to this moment. Being faithful to himself necessitated it. Everything that followed flowed from it, e.g. death, resurrection, etc. This moment is not however a segment of time. It is more a stance about life. It is an attitude of the inner person.

The meal Jesus shared with the disciples is over. It had been a very intimate time. The pace of the evening, the discourse, the praying, etc., all seem to have a sense of intensity but relaxation about them. Now the pace changes. The passion moves quickly; the events happen rapidly. There is a definite sense of urgency and drama about what is occurring. John builds the drama in many different ways. Particularly noticeable is the way his story differs from that of the synoptics in length. He completely leaves out many of the events the other evangelists recall; he includes a few new ones.

In his business-like manner John arranges the events and people and scenes that make up the passion narrative. Look at what he omits. He does not report the suffering of Gethsemani, the scene before Herod, the episode of Simon of Cyrene carrying the cross, the daughters of Jerusalem weeping as Jesus passes, Judas' death or the story of the good thief. That is a large chunk of the memory of the passion that most of us possess from our childhood.

On the other hand John includes other events that we do not find in the synoptics. He notices that the servants and attendants were standing at a coal fire warming themselves (18:18), that the Jews did not enter the praetorium (18:28), that the inscription placed over the cross by Pilate was written in three languages (19:20), etc. We need therefore to attend to the way John arranges things, to his unique view of the passion, for he has his own view of what was happening in the midst of what was going on.

The passion story, like the other themes of the gospel, has carefully been prepared for throughout the gospel. It doesn't suddenly appear on the scene. The attentive reader will have been picking up signs all along the way. The overall effect that John has managed to convey is that Jesus is carefully and deliberately moving to this moment in his life. It will also be perceived that this life of Jesus is always marked in two ways: (a) by cross–sacrifice, and (b) by gift–

freedom. Look at how the different chapters so far have subtly and not so subtly pointed to this moment:

Chapter	Event	Passion Clue
1:29	Salutation of Baptist	Lamb
2:4	Cana	Hour
2:19–22	Temple	Destroy this Temple
3:14–16	Nicodemus	Lifted Up
5:19–47	Paralytic	Whole Section
6:48–53	Eucharist	Flesh
8:28	Talking to Scribes	Revelation Through Cross
10:11	Good Shepherd	Lays Down His Life
11:46	Lazarus	Christ Condemned
12:24	Andrew	Unless Wheat Dies
12:32	Philip	Lifted Up

It can be clearly seen from the chart that John is always pointing toward this moment, that Jesus is always moving toward it, and that in fact, as he states at the last supper, he has desired it. Now the supper is over and he leaves the table with the disciples and goes out across a brook called the Kidron to a garden.

What is the name of this garden? The synoptics know of a garden called Gethsemani which is a place of great suffering, where sweat turns into blood, etc. This garden that John mentions is not a place of suffering. Perhaps that is why he omits the name Gethsemani which means "oil press." This garden that they are now entering is a place of friendship where Jesus had frequently gone with his disciples. It is presented much more as a garden of intimacy in John who now develops his story by what he leaves out and what he includes.

This garden is not a garden of agony as we find in

Mark.[1] There is no great agony, no bloody sweating, no anxious worrying about the approaching death. There is for John no Jesus prostrate on the ground begging for the chalice to pass him by. There is no sense of his being overwhelmed or frightened by the presence of a whole cohort (about six hundred men) of soldiers. The disciples are not flying away in panic, unable to watch with Jesus or pray with him. Peter who is anxious to defend Jesus is told to sheathe his sword, for there is in this garden no need for armed resistance and violence. Jesus is in charge and in control in this garden.

In this garden Jesus is the one who takes the initiative. John says, as if to underscore the point, that he "knew everything that was going to happen to him." He goes to the gate at the edge of the garden. The soldiers never do enter this place of intimate friendship. He begins the questioning process, asking them what they want as he had asked so many others in the gospel. The soldiers fall back helpless when he identifies himself. It is they, not he, who exhibit fear and anxiety. Judas does not kiss him here to point him out. Jesus identifies himself for the soldiers, so there is no confusion about whom they should arrest, and it is he who sets the terms of his capture. They are to let the rest go free. He prevents violence. He stops Peter. There is to be no action placed that prevents the coming of this hour. He welcomes this moment and has no need to be protected from it. He surrenders himself. As he said before, he is "free to lay down his life and free to take it up again." Nobody takes it from him. John concludes this garden scene with his ironic[2] touch, which indeed runs throughout the passion. He says that they came with torches. They were arresting the light of the world.

John moves the drama now to the trial before Annas. The irony continues. The guards tied Jesus up as if they

could harness the freedom of the world. Their action however serves only to highlight his freedom. Here he is still in
charge. He refuses to answer the high priest's questions. He
is content to refer him to the fact that he has always been
the life-giver who spoke the truth that set people free. He
did this in the synagogue daily. He demands proof of his
wrongdoing and they cannot present it. The guards slap
him here in a display of power, but it is obvious that Jesus
is the real leader. Notice also here how in contrast to the
synoptics there is no spitting, no game playing. Humiliation
does not belong here. John is presenting us with a scene of
exaltation.

Peter's story is made to fit into the Jesus story in an
interesting manner. He does deny Jesus, but here the denials are not placed one after the other. They are broken up
as if to lessen their impact on the reader. The first denial
takes place before the trial by Annas. The remaining two
take place after the trial by Annas and before the trial by
Pilate. Within the denials there is a buildup of resistance on
Peter's part. Even the three questioners here are different.
The first one is an anonymous girl, the second are some
slaves and servants around the fire, and the third is a relative of Malchus whose ear Peter cut off. Here also we note
that the reaction of Peter following the denials is not given.
We are left with the contrast between Peter's "I am not" in
the face of his questioners and Jesus' "I am" in the presence
of his interrogators. In John Jesus dominates the stage even
here and everyone else is present only to point to that
essential reality. Once they have done that, they can leave.
Their presence is no longer required. What happens to Peter
following the denial is therefore not important for John. He
omits any further reference. It is also interesting to note that
here the denials are different from those in the synoptics.
Here it is not the Lordship of Jesus that Peter denies but his

own discipleship. He denies that he is a follower, that he is a disciple.

Now we approach the trial before Pilate. This is central for John. Everything in the passion is arranged by him to focus on this trial, and at the center of this trial we will witness a coronation ceremony. The structure helps us understand the message, so for a moment we pause to look at the structure. Crossan[3] tells us that the whole passion has three acts: (1) 18:12–28; (2) 18:28–19:16; (3) 19:16–42. The trial before Pilate (2) is the central act. When we now turn to this act, we find that according to Crossan it has seven scenes, and these he lists as follows:

18:28–32	Outside	Authorities Demand Death
33–38	Inside	Pilate Questions
38–40	Outside	Jesus Innocent
19:1–3	Inside	Jesus Crowned King
4–8	Outside	Jesus Innocent
9–12	Inside	Pilate Questions
13–16	Outside	Authorities Obtain Death

Looking at these scenes, we can notice how the fourth scene is central. It is the cornerstone of the passion narrative, and the meaning of the passion for John radiates from it. What John is describing is in fact a coronation ceremony. This is part of John's irony, that he could so state the truth in the midst of this apparently degrading scene.

The trial begins in the "early morning" which contrasts with Judas' betrayal at "night." John tells us that the Jews refuse to enter the praetorium, which is significant because it tells us that this is the day the Passover lamb was killed and the Jews do not want to defile themselves on this day. It would have prevented their participating in the Passover meal. The crowd therefore stays outside the praetorium and

Jesus enters it alone. Now we notice the contrast that Crossan points to in the chart above between the outside and the inside, between what is happening outside the praetorium and what is going on inside.[4]

On the outside everything is a mess. There is a rather large gathering which Crossan notes is not there to condemn Jesus but to free Barrabas. On the inside Jesus is alone and calm. Pilate is in the middle. He moves back and forth from the outside to the inside. It is a position that is most appropriately his. He is in the middle and remains there throughout the trial. He is constantly vacillating back and forth. He is a chameleon trying to blend into the background, trying to avoid taking a stance, which itself becomes a stance, and eventually this non-decision becomes the decision that leads to Jesus' death. In seeking to avoid a decision Pilate has to deny what he senses, intuits and believes is the truth. Culpepper rightly observes that he is "a study in the impossibility of compromise, the inevitability of decision, and the consequences of each alternative."[5]

The interview between Pilate and Jesus would be funny if it wasn't so tragic. John's irony is at work here. He has Pilate sit on the chair of judgment, the Lithostroton,[6] passing sentence on the Savior of the world. Even the question he addresses to Jesus is ironic. He says in effect, "Don't you know that I have the power, the authority, the wherewithal, the energy and the clout to crucify you?" He is apparently so powerful and yet he is terribly lacking in confidence and freedom. In fact he makes the worst decision a judge could make—he leaves it up to the accusers. He does this in spite of the fact, or maybe because of it, that he doesn't know the crime, he doesn't believe the accusers, he proclaims Jesus innocent, he doesn't know what the truth is, he is not ready to decide, and yet he feels that he must act because of the crowd. Here then is the irony; Pilate sitting in the place of judgment and justice, proclaiming innocence and freedom in his conscious voice, and yet, because of his own unconscious bondage to Rome, to the crowd, to his position and status, condemning innocence itself to death.

Jesus stands in marked contrast to Pilate. Jesus stands; Pilate sits. Jesus is bound; Pilate appears free. Jesus is accused; Pilate is the accuser. Jesus is mocked, scourged and facing death; Pilate is lauded, hailed, and awaiting honors. Jesus is clear-sighted about his mission, his goals, his self-understanding. Pilate doesn't know who is innocent or guilty, what he believes, or what he should do. Perhaps, says D. Moody Smith, "it is too much to say that Jesus interrogates Pilate, rather than Pilate interrogating Jesus; yet it is nonetheless clear that Jesus, not Pilate, is in control of matters. Indeed Jesus' own fixity of purpose is contrasted, probably quite deliberately, with Pilate's uncertainty."[7] In this contrast it is clear that Jesus is still the central figure and that he is still in control.

The central scene now develops its most important point. Pilate crowns Jesus as King. He does this to please the crowd and the people. He gives him, in mockery, the insignia of royalty, the crown and the cloak, and then he presents him to the people for their homage and accolades. This for Pilate is mockery, but for John it is reality. Jesus is the King. In fact when he speaks now he uses terms like "my reign" and "my kingship" which is post-Easter language. He makes it clear that his kingdom is not of this world, that it is not based on political power or economic power, etc. In this way, says Benoit, John "lays bare for us the main lines of the trial: the two matters at issue, the false political one and the real religious one."[8] John proclaims Jesus King and yet clearly states that this kingdom is not brought about by, initiated by, or maintained by, power and violence. Jesus' renunciation of power is essential to the kingdom. Jesus is the witness to truth, and so for John it is "as revealer that Jesus is King because he lives entirely by the truth and communicates it. In the encounter with him people experience divine reality as liberating, redeeming love."[9]

Even when the trial is completed John is careful to show Jesus in charge of events. He is in a very real sense in the passion, as Ernst Kasemann describes him throughout the gospel, "God striding over the earth."[10] Now he carries his own cross. There is no Simon of Cyrene. He does not have to account for the daughters of Jerusalem weeping, and the two others crucified with him seem to be mainly recorded as a way of granting Jesus center stage. Jesus is still central. It is interesting to note how now in the gospel Jesus uses the words "lifted up" to refer to his crucifixion. The word is somewhat ambiguous. It can be used to describe "the act by which one is placed on a cross and crucified, but it can also be used to describe the process by which a person is enthroned as King."[11] John's irony is again at work. His executioners in putting him to death are in fact enthroning him as King. On the cross John is also careful to carry this through. He is astute in omitting the cry of anguish that reflects a sense of abandonment, a point that Mark highlights. His bones are not broken and he is not disgraced. This, John is saying, is not humiliation but glorification.

Four women and the disciple whom Jesus loved stand at the foot of the cross. In the synoptics they are at a distance. Here they are close. Interestingly neither Mary nor John is mentioned by name. One is the "beloved" disciple; the other is "Jesus' mother" and "woman." Schüssler Fiorenza says that in so addressing Mary she is "characterized as one of the apostolic women disciples" and that John "represents the disciples of Jesus who, having left everything, now receive a new familial community."[12] Jesus speaks to them from the cross but now it is not the voice of pleading. It is the voice of royalty. He is bringing his life to closure, completeness and fulfillment. He gives them to each other and then he issues his final statement: "It is finished." He brings his life to closure; no one takes it from him. He "bows his head and dies."

Above him on the cross the beat goes on. There is placed an inscription in three languages, Hebrew, Latin and Greek. These were the languages of the known world so that they point to the universalism of this kingship. This is for John the public proclamation of the coronation. Even the fact that the inscription becomes a matter of contention between Pilate and the Jews further attests to its importance. It leaves us with the necessity of decision. Is it a question of "he said" he was King of the Jews or is he "in fact" the King?

The closing scene of the passion story is itself part of the message. Jesus is laid in a tomb, and the manner in which it is referred to reveals the glory and honor to be accorded him. There is the excessive quantity of spices, about a hundred pounds in weight, which Nicodemus brings. There is the wrapping of the body in linen cloth. Linen is mentioned as opposed to wool. It was made from flax and therefore spoke to the moment of immortality. Finally there is the burial itself in a new tomb in which no one else had ever been placed. Everything about the burial appears to be special, important, and noted, for he whom they bury is special, important and to be noted. He is the King, "God striding on the earth."

This passion story reflects the choice of Jesus. It was not a momentary thing. It was not isolated from the rest of his life. It is rather the natural culmination of his whole life process. This death proclaims and manifests and validates his existence. It is here that his belief is fully incarnated and experienced. It is the concretization of his intuition, the celebration of his ultimate conviction about life. Here he makes the discovery that who he is can withstand alienation, accusation, condemnation and death. Death reveals the core of his life, it reveals who he is, and so for John it is the ultimate Christological statement: he is King and life-giver.

It is here that John proclaims love, freedom and wholeness. It is strange, ironic even, that in this bleeding, battered, shattered moment of his death, when everything appears to have fallen apart, John can now proclaim that everything holds together. This is the opposite of Yeats' line "Things fall apart the center cannot hold."[13] This is the hour for which he watched, of which he spoke as inevitable, to which he headed, and which in the scheme of things is his glory. This is the hour that he would not let anyone, least of all his disciples, keep him from meeting. It is no accident that it should be called the hour, for an hour is one full circle of the clock. It completes the circle. It brings it to fullness and wholeness. Jung calls it a mandala. In this hour the cross and the circle hold together.

The passion is my story also. I see in it not only the culmination of the gospel but through it the gathering of all the facets of my own personality. They are all there. Judas is here in the love of silver, the love of money, a desire that can lead me astray much quicker than any frontal attack on my own sense of wholeness. I see the crowd. I know how I would like to join the crowd and move with them, even their violence, rather than join the inner hero in the battle against the faces of the dragon. It is easier to remain in the anonymity of the group, a willing victim of cultural consciousness strutting through life with a sense of detached arrogance. The crowd milieu covers my desire to bind truth and harness freedom. I recognize myself too in the many images of Peter in the passion. First he is the impulsive one whose impulsivity leads him to violence without his understanding what Jesus is all about. It brings me in touch with my own impulsiveness that leads to violence. Then he keeps me in touch with my own denials which are really a refusal to be attentive to the clues toward wholeness offered in the journey of life. The denial is really a refusal to follow the leadership of the emergent self, a desire to hold back, to live a partial existence.

Even more pointed is the Pilate dimension of my existence. I move inward and outward looking for clues to judgment, looking for a way out of responsibility. It is the "puer aeternus" in me trying to wash my hands of adult responsibility, handing over to others the decision about my inner life. Inside proclaims innocence, outside demands condemnation, and all the while I ignore the feminine ally that is available, which if I would but listen to could help me in the process of decision making. To stay in touch with her would be to stay in tune with one who knows the way out. I recognize myself in the voice that cries, "Do with him as you want." This is the abandonment of my inner life.

But this is not the whole story. I see myself not only in the many people who interact with Jesus but also in the Jesus who goes to the cross of freedom, in the one who goes forth to meet his hour. In these moments I have a sense of the opposites of my life coming together, being held together in creative tension. It is as if I take the opposites within, and they are held together by something, or someone, larger that lies in the inner depths of my being, and out of this a newer me begins to emerge that is continuous with the old me but now is somehow stronger. There are moments when I know the cross itself. I know exactly where the vertical and horizontal bars meet. The vertical bar reaches up to the sky, to the light, to consciousness. It is the masculine pole of my existence. The vertical bar also reaches down into the depths, the dark, the earth, the unconscious. It grounds my being. It is the feminine pole of my life, the reservoir of life itself. The horizontal bars reach out to embrace the universe left and right of me. It touches the criminal, the inferior parts, the unacceptable impulses, feelings, and attitudes that surround my being. It gathers and heals the broken, cut-off isolated parts of my humanity.

In the passion story I begin to recognize my life. I come to see it not only as old but as new, not only as partial but as total, not only as death but as life. I see my life and have a sense of joy in the midst of it all. I recall Henri Nouwen's lines: "Joy is always new. Whereas there can be old pain, old grief, and old sorrow, there can be no old joy. Old joy is not joy. Joy is always connected with movement, renewal, rebirth, change . . . in short, with life."[14] This cross, this passion, this Christ within comes to its hour, and it does so with a hope and a sense that my life too can be a coronation in freedom in which cross and circle hold together.

Chapter 18
John 20:1—20:20
From Extraordinary to Ordinary

It is Eastertime right now in the parish as I write the concluding chapters of this book. It's a nice time to be writing on the resurrection stories because we are hearing them daily in the liturgy. Listening to them now makes me aware again of how difficult it must have been for the early disciples to realize what had happened. True, they had been prepared for it and warned that it would happen, but it's so unbelievable that it doesn't fit into our normal kind of logic. How do you make sense out of an empty tomb? The logical thing is to say that someone took the body, or hid it, or something like that; in fact, it seems that the resurrection stories were in part constructed to deal with that problem. The fact that the tomb was empty must have been a challenge to their reasoning in the beginning. It still is for many people.

Our difficulties are probably of a slightly different order, or at least so it appeared to me as I heard the different accounts of the four evangelists read in the past week.

There are so many contradictions in the stories. There are a lot of gaps, a lot of duplications with shifts in the data, oddities in the reports, etc. It's not just that these are minor differences, but, viewed from one vector, the four evangelists don't appear to agree on too much, at least on first hearing. Matthew, for instance, says that Mary Magdalene and the other Mary went to the grave to see it. Mark agrees that two women went to the grave, but he says that it was Mary and Salome and that the reason they went was to anoint the body. Luke agrees with the fact that women went to the grave, but says that it was a "number" of women and he doesn't give us their names. He does, however, agree that they went to anoint the body. John says that it was only one woman who went, and he says nothing about the anointing since he already has the body anointed before the last supper.

Further confusion is added when they get to the grave, whenever that was, because on that they also differ. Matthew says that it was after the sabbath as Sunday morning was dawning; Mark says that it was early on Sunday morning, at sunrise; Luke says that it was early on Sunday morning; John says that it was early on Sunday morning but while it was still dark. At the grave Matthew tells us that they saw an angel; Mark says it was a young man; Luke says it was two young men; John says it was two angels.

There is then a great deal of confusion in the different reports, but, as others have pointed out, the evangelists are writing from different perspectives and organize their material accordingly. Our journey is with John who gives us five stories about the resurrection. There are the empty tomb story, the appearance to Mary, the appearance to the disciples, and the appearance to Thomas with which the gospel is brought to a close. All of these stories center on Jerusalem. A subsequent story about an appearance to Peter and the disciples on the lake was later introduced to form the Galilee tradition. We will deal with this story in the last chapter, making only general references to it here.

John's gospel closes with these five stories, which we notice do not include any mention of the ascension and the feast of Pentecost. Initially that may surprise us since our liturgical calendar is modeled more on the Lukan narrative. In consequence there is an interval of forty and fifty days between these celebrations in our liturgical calendar. John has no such interval. The resurrection-ascension-Pentecost sequence is all one event for him. Schillebeeckx says that "the dying and death are not a precondition to be followed by the resurrection in the form of a reward,"[1] but rather that "for John going to the Father is a single event, death, resurrection, Easter gift."[2] John therefore presents the outpouring of the Spirit in these stories. Mary, for instance, comes to the grave weeping, but, as Jesus promised, now her weeping is turned into joy. The disciples are called my brothers and their Father is his Father which is a fulfillment of the last supper's promise. They too now experience the greeting of peace which was his farewell gift to them, and through them the world will experience it. The Spirit is breathed on them. Thomas is led into truth, again fulfilling a promise that the Spirit would come and lead them into all truth.

These five stories seem to have a few basic experiences in common and indeed we find threads of them appearing in the other accounts. In these stories fight and flight as responses seems to get a lot of attention. Mary, when she discovers the empty tomb, runs to Peter and John; Thomas runs away from the community to hide somewhere; Peter runs away to go back to fishing. The apostles run away into an upper room and board the doors. Jesus, however, is consistent. He comes and wishes them peace. It is what he has always been telling them: Don't be afraid; be at peace. He told them that when the angel first appeared to Mary in Luke's gospel. He told them that when they fell asleep in the boat. He reinforced it at the last supper and he renews it now after the resurrection.

Gradually as I notice this, it dawns on me that these people are not doing anything that is really unusual. In fact they are doing very ordinary things. Mary is on her way to the tomb, involved in an appropriate expression of grief just after the death of the one she loved. The apostles are gathered together, probably in a similar venture. Luke gives us an example of two of them on the road to Emmaus discussing all that happened in the past few days. Peter the practical man has gone back to doing what he was at previously. He has gone fishing. None of them is doing anything unusual, not even Thomas who grieves alone.

It was in this circumstance of the ordinary that they all met the risen Lord, and they met him in different guises. Mary who is a very earthy woman, wise to the ways of the world if we believe Luke, meets him as a gardener, in a very earthy way. Peter the fisherman experiences him as a fisherman who knows where the shoal can be found and directs him toward it. The disciples who throughout the gospel were so frequently the ones who misunderstood what he was saying, etc., and are constantly depicted in the gospel either staying with him or abandoning him, meet him as a wounded healer who exposes his brokenness to them, and Thomas meets him in a fleshed experience of brokenness.

Then as I listen to the stories, another point jumps right out at me. I had never quite seen it before, but it has always been there staring me in the face. All of those who met him and encountered him were called out. They experienced a sense of command or mission, and again it was not the same for each of them. It is true that the empty tomb story has no requirement, but that in itself is significant, for, as Schillebeeckx points out, "there is no belief in the Resurrection without Easter grace and an empty tomb is still not an Easter experience."[3] But look at the other stories. Mary is told something quite extraordinary but to appreciate it let me back up a moment. In the accounts of the other evangelists it was the angel at the tomb who proclaimed the Easter message. He is not here. He is risen. That is not true in John. Rather when Mary recognizes the teacher because he called her by name, she is told, "Go to my brothers and tell them—I am ascending to my Father and your Father, to my God and your God." Blank comments, "The expression 'my brothers' is a striking one. Here it connotes the new relationship Jesus now has to his disciples as he expressly includes them in his own relationship to God."[4] From my point of view it is a very definite responsibility that is now being called forth in her and given to her by the risen Lord. She is even called by name, bringing back to my mind the story of the Good Shepherd who knows his sheep. Here her response to the disciples is, "I have seen the Lord," and the importance of that is readily perceived by all that we have previously said about "seeing" and being called to "see" in the gospel.

The apostles have a similar experience. When Jesus meets them he informs them that they are now to be agents of reconciliation and that the healing of the cosmos is to an extent dependent on their activity. They are told, "As the Father has sent me, so I send you," which models their mission on his, and that "if you forgive men's sins they are forgiven them; if you do not forgive them they are not forgiven." Segovia[5] suggests that the community's mission is narrated in their immediate declaration to Thomas upon his return after he had left them. They say that they have "seen" the Lord, and again we notice the word "seen" and its importance here. They receive therefore a healing mission, and if they are willing to accept it, the cosmos in them can know a healing, reconciling presence, a peace presence. Both Thomas and Peter know a similar calling to mission. In Thomas' case it is a mission to be the believer who gives up doubt and moves on to greater faith; in Peter's case it is the mission of feeding the lambs and taking care of the sheep. At the start of the gospel they had all been called, and here now in the resurrection stories they are specifically being sent to be missionaries to themselves, to each other, and to the world.

The resurrection stories keep sounding in my ears in these days. Over and again I notice the fears, the ordinary things that the apostles are doing, the sudden appearance of the risen one and the consequent mission and mandate. But perhaps it is time now to go from the more general to the more particular and to focus on one of the stories. The one I choose is that of Thomas. It is only in John's gospel that this story is recalled, and originally it served as a fitting and climactic close to the gospel.

The story can be perceived as reflecting three tenses or moments in Thomas' life:[6]

(a) *Verses 24–26* describe what Thomas was like in the past. He is someone who followed Jesus but liked to keep him at a distance. He also stays a little removed from the disciples. It is true that he calls on them in the Lazarus story to follow Jesus to Jerusalem even if it means their death, but on the other hand he has not penetrated below the surface of Jesus' identity. He does not really know him. He doesn't even know at the last supper where Jesus is going and therefore wonders how he could possibly know the way. He is the one who in the resurrection sequences wants to maintain a rigid and isolating independence. He will not accept the testimony of others, he refuses the teaching and preaching of the witnessing church, and he insists upon his own verification through the extraordinary and the miraculous. Unless he sees the scars of the nails in his hands and puts his fingers in those scars and his hand into Jesus' side, he will not believe no matter who tells him otherwise.

(b) *Verses 26–28* show us a second phase—what Thomas is like in the present situation. John tells us that this gathering took place a week later, which would make it a Sunday again. He gives us enough evidence to conclude that the setting is a liturgical one. The disciples have gathered, the peace is shared, the Lord is present. Significantly enough, on this occasion John does not mention the presence of any fear, and because we have seen that this is John's Pentecost we understand that this is because the Spirit has been given. Fear, therefore, has given way to rejoicing. Thomas is confronted by Jesus. The confrontation takes the form of a triple invitation which ultimately leads to total conversion. Thomas' invitation involves his finger, his hand and his heart, and we could allegorize it into his physical, emotional and willful life. Whether we do or not, it is clear that the confrontation involves Thomas' total person. In the present liturgical context (remember what we said about Tabernacles[7]) Thomas is one who is faced with choice.

(c) *Verses 28–30* show us what Thomas will be in the future. We note that Thomas never did get his wish for the miraculous. He never did put his finger, hand or heart into the wounds of Christ. He comes ultimately then to Jesus not by the route of the miraculous but by the route of the ordinary. Here Thomas does not represent the group of apostles at all, as his absence from the community in the first story shows, but as Segovia suggests he "represents a different group altogether, namely those who have not witnessed Jesus' return but who are asked to accept it on the testimony of others."[8] Thomas represents therefore those who in the future come to Jesus not in confrontation with the extraordinary but through faith. He comes through doubt and questioning to faith and so Kysar says that "doubt" is for Thomas the "threshold of faith."[9]

Thomas' response at this point therefore provides for John the climactic moment of the gospel. He expresses in his reply—"My Lord and my God"—the response that John hoped to evoke in his own community and in future generations. In Thomas' reply there is for John the full and total expression of faith. For this reason, as Blank indicates, "the confessional formula at this point in John's gospel includes the two highest titles of dignity that there can be for Jesus in the New Testament, namely the titles of God and Kyrios or Lord."[10]

I come now before this scene of John's gospel in prayer. I identify with Thomas on a number of different levels. First, he is a twin and so am I. Second, he is a very physical, sensual, and incarnational kind of person, and I am very much like that also. Third, he is a doubter. It is not the word with which I would identify myself, although others have used it periodically of me. (Some say that it is natural for an Irishman to answer a question with a question; others maintain that it is because we are an obstinate race.) The word I would use would be "suspicious." That of course leaves me open to the accusation of being paranoid, but there are worse things in life than that. I suppose it depends on how you see Thomas' doubt, my suspicion. Is it negative or positive, valuable or meaningless?

As I look at Thomas in the story I come more and more to value him. Thomas knows that people, and that means disciples as well, with the best of intentions are not only authentic but also inauthentic. He reflects in the presence of the group what I consider a healthy suspicion of their testimony. It has been somewhat customary to knock Thomas for that attitude, but I admire it. Is it a blessing or a curse? It appears to me that it is a blessing. Thomas wants to know that his surrender is not abdication; that he can surrender when it is appropriate is clear in the response he gives to Jesus.

Paul Ricoeur[11] speaks of a culture of suspicion and a culture of consent existing within the larger culture. The disciples might be said to represent the latter and Thomas the former. He is suspicious of reports and situations. He knows reporters better than we who read the daily papers. He even knows consciousness and he is suspicious of that. He recognizes that he is not the only one who brings a set of biases, ambitions, fears and greeds to the situation; so also do even the well-motivated reporters of the disciples. He acknowledges, therefore, the possibility not only of his own blindness but also of theirs. Thomas wants his faith to be grounded, and he knows that there is all the difference in the world between being a sucker and being a person of faith. It seems to me that he wishes to avoid the one as much as he desires the other.

It is, however, to Thomas' credit that he not only was a man of suspicion but also was a man of consent, of affirmation, and that he can join the community of consent when it is appropriate. Confronted in the liturgical experience with the presence of the risen Lord, the presence of transcendent love, he need not push this suspicion to the edge of the ridiculous. He can let it go. In short it seems to me that he knows both its value and its limits and moves comfortably between them. Perhaps it is the tension of these opposites in balance that makes Thomas so important a figure for me now. Instead of seeing him negatively as a man of doubt, as the past has cast him because of his questioning the certainty of others, I see him now more as the man of the future who arrives at spiritual integration and confesses Jesus as Lord.

Tad Dunne[12] speaks of spiritual integration as the capacity to move meaningfully between five levels of meaning which he says are: the realm of common-sense, theory, method, religious transcendence, and story. He concludes: "The spiritually integrated person overcomes the division of the split soul because he or she understands the aims and techniques of both common-sense practicality and theoretical analysis. But beyond healing that split spiritual integration allows a person to ground all the workings of the mind and all the practical decisions of a responsible life in the love of divine mystery."[13] Thomas is for me such a person.

Chapter 19
John 21:1—21:24
From Agape to Philo

John's gospel ends with a chapter that is one of the most discussed among exegetes. The chapter is variously described by them as an addendum to the gospel, an epilogue, a postscript, or an appendix, or even by use of the phrase "a supplementary chapter."[1] It all depends on how you see the chapter as related to the main body of the gospel. It is an important chapter in helping to deal with the issues of origin and authorship. Some scholars maintain that the author is not John, while others would go even further and suggest he wasn't even a disciple of the evangelist. While exegetes discuss these questions and the consequences of their resolution, we shall move in a different direction. There are three fairly clearly defined sections to the chapter: (1) Peter and the fishing expedition, (2) Peter and Jesus; (3) Peter and the beloved disciple. I shall follow this sequence and keep Peter as the focus.

The first section is considered by Blank as an Easter story, "which is meant primarily as a peg on which to hang

191

the following two sections."[2] It is a marvelous story which
allows for identifications in many ways. It is at once a story
of success and failure, of an individual and a community, of
friendship and loneliness, of depression and exaltation.
John himself introduces the story to us as one of the "self-
revelation" of Jesus which occurs by the Lake of Tiberias. It
is therefore for him a story that tells something of Jesus. It
is also a story of Peter and the other apostles. In fact there
are seven of them gathered together: Thomas the twin who
seemed to have difficulty accepting Jesus' divinity, Nathanael the model Israelite in whom Jesus says there is no guile,
the sons of Zebedee whom John does not mention any-
where else in his gospel but whom the synoptics identify as
James and John, and finally two unknown and unnamed
disciples. There are then gathered the known and the
unknown, those who were promised greater things and
those who had difficulty accepting them, and with them is
Peter, who is apparently their leader, who gathers the community together.

Peter is an important part of this scene. He is not in
John's gospel the spokesperson for the disciples as he is in
the synoptics. Nevertheless he is a leader. He has decided
upon a course of action and they have followed. He has
decided in the light of Jesus' death to go fishing. He goes
back to doing what he had been doing before he met Jesus.
Peter is a doer and he appears to find some consolation in
work, so he goes to work. John makes special mention of
the fact that Peter goes back to work at night. It fits in with
his whole emphasis on darkness. Judas too had gone out
from the supper into the night. Peter had denied the light
three times, or rather he had denied that he was a follower
of the light. Now he goes back to the dark. And he doesn't
go alone. He brings the other six with him.

Fishing, however, was not the answer for Peter. There

was something wrong. Work was no longer fruitful or meaningful. They labored all night and caught nothing. The night was empty, work was empty, Peter was empty. It is into this situation of emptiness that a stranger comes. At least Peter doesn't know who the figure on the shore is. He cannot identify him. The appearance of the stranger here is not unlike the appearance of the stranger in Luke 24 as the apostles are on the way to Emmaus.[3] This stranger takes the initiative. He shouts out to the people in the boat, using the familiar form of address. This stranger is the host; he is in charge. As in the body of the gospel with his words and his questions, so now also his observations reveal, expose, and direct. His words reveal what is hidden, for from his vantage point on shore he can see the shoal of fish which they in the boat cannot. His question exposes their failure, for they have caught nothing all night. His command redirects their action. He knows what they don't, and he can tell them how, and where, to find what they are looking for in vain. He tells them that they are searching on the wrong side. They must throw out their nets on the opposite side.

When he speaks, John recognizes him. He passes on the information to Peter. This was not the first time this had happened. John was also the one who could perceive the meaning of the empty tomb in 20:8 when Peter didn't. "Simon Peter remains important but he is not the one really attuned to Jesus."[4] John's energy is reflective. Peter's is impulsive. He puts on his clothes and jumps into the water. He swims to shore. Again he is not alone. He carries a whole net full of fish with him. He is a charismatic leader. Coming to the shore he meets Jesus who invites him to breakfast. They were dependent on him during the night; now they are still dependent on him, but they have a contribution to make. He invites them to bring some of their own catch. He takes what is theirs and adds what is his. The two together make the meal that they will share. What they had taken from the water becomes their nourishment, but only after he had taken it and blessed it and given it to them. The actions of Jesus are highlighted and emphasized here. It is, says Schnackenburg, "his words, his actions, his gestures which are important. He, Jesus, is the host; he is absolutely central, and the disciples know it is the Lord."[5]

The story opens me to a lot of questions when I consider it as a story of self. How have I gone back to fishing in my life? Why do I only fish on one side of the boat? What is it like to discover that the significant relationship is gone from my life? How does its loss move me to action? What is it like to discover now that my life is fruitless? Why can't I recognize the Lord? What are the obstacles in the way? Who is John in my life who hears what I cannot? What is it like when he has to tell me? What is it like to hear the familiar voice from the shore? What is the water in my life into which I must put the net to become fruitful? What is it like to jump into the water? What is it like to come to shore? The questions keep coming, opening me to the various aspects of the story in me, and yet it is not over. The gospel goes on.

Jesus comes to Peter. Out of the silence of the shared meal comes a new conversation. Shared life raises the inevitable question of relationship. How are Jesus and Peter related? Who are they vis-à-vis each other? It's the key question. Three times Peter had denied his own discipleship and therefore their relationship and friendship. This meeting now must be so that things can be clarified again. There is a heavy tone to the meeting, as is evidenced in the very strict formula with which Jesus speaks to Peter. Jesus still is in charge. The question he asks Peter is at once very simple and complex. "Do you love me?" has many meanings. Significantly, in the dialogue between Jesus and Peter, we see that the question itself, although asked three times, undergoes change each time. To understand that, I have reprinted here the interchange between the two with the significant passages underlined:

Jesus: Simon, son of John, do you *love* me *(agapais)*
        more than these others do?
Peter: Yes, Lord, you know that *I love (philo)* you.
Jesus: Feed my lambs. Simon, son of John, do you
        love me *(Agapais)?*
Peter: Yes, Lord, you know that I *love (philo)* you.
Jesus: Tend my sheep. Simon, son of John, do you
        love me (philais)?
Peter: Lord, you know everything. You know that
        I love (philo) you.
Jesus: Feed my sheep.

In his study of this passage Ceslaus Spicq notices that in the second question Jesus leaves out the words "more than these others" contained in the first question and that in the third question Jesus uses a different word (the same one Peter uses) for love than he did in the first two questions. He then goes on to say; "Agapan refers not to a love that is more rational and voluntary than Philein but to love in the technical sense it had in the Septuagint: religious attachment and consecration to God expressing itself on the moral plane by total fidelity and obedience in the exclusive service of the Lord. . . . Jesus asked of Peter both charity and the virtue of religion which expresses itself in devotion to the interests of the Lord."[6] What Peter answers is *philo,* which is a word that expresses the kind of love one person has for another. It is not totally disinterested love. It still has a "strong egotistical attachment."[7] Jesus here then, it seems, is asking of Peter more than Peter is either able or willing to give, but in the end Jesus accepts that which Peter can give. Peter promises to Jesus all the natural tenderness and affection that friends can give to each other, and Jesus accepts that from him.

In the course of the exchange Jesus also entrusts to Peter the care of the flock. Some have pointed out that Peter doesn't own the flock. Jesus still retains ownership, but he commissions Peter to care for them. Catholic and Protestant scholars tend to interpret this and related Petrine passages differently and so tend to view the concept of authority in the church differently.[8] They would agree, however, that here Peter is given the responsibility of the care of the sheep. There is an "implicit patterning of Peter the Shepherd on Jesus the Good Shepherd"[9] so that if Peter is to feed the sheep it implies that he will have to give his life for them. Here then the function of shepherd is again associated with the twin concepts of love and death as it had been in chapter 10 in the Good Shepherd story. It is interesting to note that it is only when Peter has affirmed his love and friendship for Jesus and received the commission from him to feed the flock knowing that it would involve death that he is invited to follow. When he was young he could do what he wanted, and go where he wanted, but maturity is characterized by responsibility. It's the same Peter, but now others have a claim on him; they have put a belt around him and led him where, left to himself, he would not go.

The chapter's third scene brings together Peter and "that other disciple, the one whom Jesus loved, the one who leaned close to Jesus at the meal." Many have sought to discover who this person is and whether he was in fact a real historical figure or not. It seems now that the consensus of opinion is that this person is John and that he was a real historical person.[10] Be that a matter of conjecture or not, it is still true to say that the beloved disciple of the gospel is portrayed as the ideal disciple. He has what Culpepper calls a "representative, paradigmatic and symbolic significance . . . who has no misunderstandings."[11] Apparently there were two strong groups in existence at the time the gospel was composed, and each was tracing its lineage and tradition to Jesus, one group through Peter and the other through John. The gospel of John presses its claim by placing in what some call conflict, and others relationship, these two strong figureheads. Schnackenburg says that it is not "immediately permissible to interpret the competition between the two as rivalry."[12] Their relationship is perceived and developed in the scenes in which they appear together. Some of those scenes come back into focus now as we face the final scene. In review we can notice how at the last supper John can ask of Jesus what Peter cannot concerning who will betray him. John can follow Jesus to the cross while Peter gets sidetracked in denial. John gets to the tomb first but then waits for Peter. John perceives the meaning of the empty tomb first but then he informs Peter. On the Lake of Tiberias John sees Jesus and recognizes the Lord, while Peter does not. However it is Peter who jumps into the water and carries the net full of fish to the shore. Peter proclaims his love for Jesus following the morning breakfast, but the author is careful to note, through the arrangement of the questions, that it is no greater than "that of these others," among whom is John.

The two now appear together again in these last scenes of the gospel and they appear with Jesus. There is evidently a reason for their being together in conflict, rivalry or relationship. Now Peter turns around and sees the disciple whom Jesus loved following him. He inquires of Jesus what John's fate will be in the future. In reply he is told in effect to mind his own business. The Lord has something special in mind for John, and Peter is to respect that calling. Two

points seem significant here. First, Peter seems to be given
to comparison. He wants to know how John is going to be
treated. Peter is again on the border of hesitation, nearly
ready to forget the call to follow a second time and to judge
himself on what will happen to John. Jesus therefore confronts him immediately: "How does that concern you?" He
invites Peter to clarify his own gifts and reasons for following. The second point flows from it as Jesus continues
speaking. There are different ways of following Jesus and
each must be respected. One way is the way of the martyr,
the way of Peter; the other is the way of "remaining," the
way of John. Blank makes the following observation: "Peter
and certainly many other disciples as well had died a martyr's death, like Jesus himself. Beyond a doubt this gave
them a high reputation as radical followers. . . . But what if
there were disciples of Jesus who had followed him from
the first hour but who had reached old age and did not die
a martyr's death. . . . Both ways of following are good ones.
We must let Jesus decide which way will lead the individual
disciple, for the same way is not suited to all."[13]

As I enter this chapter seeing it as a story of self, I am
struck by the presence of Peter. How often I think he has
surfaced in my own life in all of his impulsivity, wanting to
jump into the water, cut off people's ears, or agree too
quickly with some requirement without understanding the
values involved. I recognize him in the times I have acted
without an awareness of the price required and without any
consideration of whether I was either ready or willing to
pay the price. I recognize him within those moments where
I compare myself with others, wanting to know what they
are doing and whether they are doing more or less, better
or worse. I see his face within me in the unhealthy and negative competitiveness that marks my behavior. But the
chapter also puts me in touch with a deeper self within, a

Christ self, that has a more cosmic view of life, that sees things in their totality, that wishes to draw me beyond my psychic infancy. The deeper self reveals to me how narrow I still am, how confined I am within limited areas of thinking, and it calls me to love and care for the fragmentary parts of my existence even as it points out the way to something larger. After all Peter, as Elizabeth Bowden Howes points out, "did many things but he never ran away. His ambiguity and ambivalence are consistently shown, but he stayed with the central value. . . . [He had] an ability to perceive those qualities in Jesus against which he saw himself as simple and partial. The fact that he could see the contrast was because he had both things in himself . . . partialness and potential wholeness."[14]

As I look to Peter and listen to the self within, I discover that the self-revelation of the holy is both threatening and freeing. It invites me to follow without comparison and competition but with faith in the larger vision that I cannot see. It invites me to trust my own experience without negating any other person's experience, to value my own calling without denying any other person's calling, and to live graciously in the midst of diversity. Discovering this is discovering that the transformation is not completed, that there is much more for me to hear, and much more of me that will be revealed even though I cannot hear it as yet. It will take more time for this to happen. It will take a lifetime. In the meantime my calling is to continue journeying within the transcendent.

Notes

Introduction

1. Matthew 1:1–18.
2. Mark 1:9–14.
3. Luke 1:1—4:20.
4. John 1:1.
5. Raymond Brown, *The Gospel According to John: Volume I*, Anchor Bible 29, Doubleday, Garden City, N.Y., 1966, p. 18.
6. T. S. Eliot, *Four Quartets:* "Dry Salvages," Harcourt, Brace and World, Inc., N.Y., 1971, 1 211, p. 44.
7. R. Alan Culpepper, *Anatomy of the Fourth Gospel: A Study in Literary Design*, Fortress Press, Philadelphia, 1983, p. 104.
8. Ibid., p. 106.
9. Nils Alstrup Dahl, *Jesus in the Memory of the Early Church*, Augsburg Publishing House, Minneapolis, 1976, p. 119.
10. J. Louis Martyn, *Glimpses into the History of the Johannine Community: The Gospel of John in Christian History*, Paulist Press, N.J., 1979, pp. 90–121.
    J. Louis Martyn, *History and Theology in the Fourth Gospel*, Harper and Row, N.Y., 1968.
11. Cf. comments on Pancaro's work by Robert Kysar, "Community and Gospel: Vectors in Fourth Gospel Criticism," in *Interpreting the Gospels*, J. Luther Mays, ed., Fortress Press, Philadelphia, 1981, p. 273.

12. Jerome Neyrey, *Christ Is Community: Christologies of the New Testament*, Michael Glazier, Delaware, 1985, pp. 142ff.
13. Diarmuid McGann, *The Journeying Self: The Markan Gospel in a Jungian Perspective*, Paulist Press, N.J., 1985.

Chapter 1—John: 1—1:18

1. Raymond Brown, *The Gospel According to John: Volume I*, op. cit., p. 23.
2. Rudolf Schnackenburg, *The Gospel According to St. John, Volume I*, Herder and Herder, 1968, pp. 226ff.
3. Ibid.
4. John Tauler, "Sermon on the Three Births of Christmas," in *The Soul Afire: Revelations of the Mystics*, M. A. Reinhold, ed., Doubleday, N.Y., 1973, p. 451.
5. R. Alan Culpepper, *Anatomy of the Fourth Gospel: A Study in Literary Design*, op. cit., p. 88.
6. Raymond Brown, *The Gospel According to John: Volume I*, op. cit., p. 4.
7. Cf. Richard Woods, O.P., *Eckhart's Way: The Way of the Christian Mystics*, Vol. II, Michael Glazier, Delaware, 1986, p. 92.
8. Matthew Fox, *Breakthrough: Meister Eckhart's Creation Spirituality*, in new translation, Image Books, Doubleday, Garden City, N.Y., 1980, pp. 56–82.
9. Ibid.
10. John Painter, *Reading John's Gospel Today*, John Knox Press, Atlanta, 1975, p. 33.
11. Ezekiel 37:27.
12. Joel 3:1.
13. Pierre Teilhard De Chardin, *The Divine Milieu*, Harper and Row, N.Y., 1960, p. 89.
14. Thomas Merton, *New Seeds of Contemplation*, New Directions, N.Y., 1961, pp. 35–36.
15. Thomas Berry, *Classical American Spirituality and the American Experience*, Riverdale Papers VII, Riverdale Center for Religious Research, N.Y., p. 13.

Chapter 2—John 1:19—2:1

1. Raymond Brown, *The Gospel According to John: Volume I*, op. cit., p. cxxxix.
2. Rudolf Schnackenburg, *The Gospel According to St. John*, Vol. I, op. cit., p. 284.
3. Raymond Brown, *The Gospel According to John: Volume I*, op. cit., pp. 58ff.
4. Robert Kysar, *John the Maverick Gospel*, John Knox Press, Atlanta, 1976, p. 32.
5. R. Alan Culpepper, *Anatomy of the Fourth Gospel: A Study in Literary Design*, op. cit., p. 133.
6. Cf. Rudolf Schnackenburg, *The Gospel According to St. John*, Vol. I, op. cit., p. 310.
7. Paul S. Minear, "The Audience of the Fourth Evangelist," in *Interpreting the Gospels*, James Mays, ed., Fortress Press, Philadelphia, 1981, p. 258.
8. Elizabeth Bowden Howes and Sheila Moon, *Man the Choicemaker*, Westminster Press, Philadelphia, 1973, p. 79.

Chapter 3—John 2:1—2:12

1. John Dominic Crossan, O.S.M., *The Gospel of Eternal Life: Reflections on the Theology of St. John*, Bruce Publishing, Milwaukee, 1967, p. 54.
2. Rosemary Haughton, *The Passionate God*, Paulist Press, New Jersey, 1981, pp. 176ff.
3. John Sanford, *Fritz Kunkel: Selected Writings*, Paulist Press, New Jersey, 1984.
4. I include here a list of some of the more important references to the life-giving hour of Christ in John:

Incident	Chapter	Key Word
Cana	2:4	Hour
Temple	2:19	Destroy Temple
Nicodemus	3:14	Lifted Up
Paralytic	5:19	Whole Section

Eucharist	6:48–53	Flesh Given
Scribes	8:28	Revelation Through Cross
Shepherd	10:10	Lays Down
Lazarus	11:25	Condemned as Lifegiver
Philip and Andrew	12:24	Unless Wheat Dies

5. Rudolf Schnackenburg, *The Gospel According to St. John*, Vol. I, op. cit., p. 339.
6. Edward Schillebeeckx, *Christ*, Seabury Press, N.Y., 1980.
7. Raymond Brown, *The Gospel According to John: Volume I*, op. cit., p. 530.
8. Elisabeth Schüssler Fiorenza offers the following comment on the response of Jesus to his mother: "The address distances Jesus from his biological mother and rejects any claim she may have had on him because of her family relationship to him. At the same time it places Mary of Nazareth at the same level as the Samaritan woman and Mary of Magdala, both of whom were apostolic witnesses and exemplary disciples. . . . The leaders of the community were admonished to do whatever he tells you . . . by a woman disciple": *In Memory of Her: A Feminist Theological Reconstruction of Christian Origins*, Crossroad, N.Y., 1984, p. 327.
9. Edward Schillebeeckx, *Christ*, op. cit., p. 325.
10. Nathan Schwartz Salant, *Narcissism and Character Transformation: The Psychology of Narcissistic Character Disorders*, Inner City Books, Toronto, 1982, p. 67.
11. Marie Louise Von Franz, *Puer Aeternus: A Psychological Study of the Adult Struggle with the Paradise of Childhood*, Sigo Press, 1981, pp. 220–221.

Chapter 4—John 2:12—3:1

1. Rudolf Schnackenburg, *The Gospel According to St. John*, Vol. I, op. cit., p. 345.
2. Roger Corless, *I Am Food*, Crossroad, N.Y., 1981, p. 29.
3. Stephen Kaung, *The Songs of Degrees*, Christian Fellowship Publishers, N.Y., 1970.

4. Diarmuid McGann, *The Journeying Self: The Gospel of Mark Through a Jungian Perspective*, op. cit., pp. 130ff.
5. Cf. John L. McKenzie, *Dictionary of the Bible*, Bruce Publishing, Milwaukee, 1965, pp. 426ff. Also cf. *The Jerome Biblical Commentary*, Brown, Fitzmyer, Murphy, ed., Prentice-Hall, Englewood Cliffs, N.J., Vol. 2, 1973, pp. 93ff.
6. Genesis 14.
7. Matthew 23:37.
8. Ezekiel 16 and 23.
9. Bernhard Andersen, *The Living World of the Old Testament*, Longman Green, London, 1957, pp. 368–369.
10. Revelation 21:2.
11. John Huckle and Paul Visokay, "The Gospel According to John," Vol. I, *The New Testament for Spiritual Reading*, No. 7, John McKenzie, ed., Crossroad, N.Y., 1981, p. 31.
12. Raymond Brown, *The Gospel According to John*, Volume I, op. cit., p. 123.
13. Jerome Neyrey, *Christ Is Community: Christologies of the New Testament*, op. cit., p. 159.
14. Carl Gustav Jung, "Answer to Job: Psychology and Religion West and East," Vol. II, *Collected Works*, trans. R.F.C. Hull, Bollingen Series XX, 1958, p. 416.
15. William F. Lynch, *Images of Hope*, University of Notre Dame Press, 1974, p. 233.
16. T. S. Eliot, *Four Quartets*, "Dry Salvages," op. cit., line 214.
17. Ibid.

Chapter 5—John 3:1—4:1

1. John 3:1ff; 7:50; 19:39.
2. R. Alan Culpepper, *Anatomy of the Fourth Gospel: A Study in Literary Design*, op. cit., p. 136.
3. Richard Viladesau, *The Reason for Our Hope*, Paulist Press, N.J., 1984, p. 116.
4. Martin Heidegger, *Discourse on Thinking*, John Anderson and E. Hans Freund, trans., Harper Books, N.Y., 1966, p. 46.
5. Rudolf Schnackenburg, *The Gospel According to St. John*, Vol. I, op. cit., p. 366.

6. Robert Kysar, *The Scandal of Lent*, Augsburg, Minneapolis, 1982, p. 11.

7. R. Alan Culpepper, *Anatomy of the Fourth Gospel: A Study in Literary Design*, op. cit., p. 135.

8. Peter Mann has written, using the hermeneutics of Paul Ricoeur, of the "journey through the image as movement from spectator to scientific observer to existential participant to seer." I am indebted to him for sharing with me his insights on this and I have collaborated with him on many programs flowing from it. For further study of his work, cf. *Spirituality and Innervision: Studies in Formative Spirituality*, Vol. I, No. 1, February 1980, pp. 103–114.

9. John Dunne, *The Reasons of the Heart: A Journey into Solitude and Back Again into the Human Circle*, University of Notre Dame Press, 1978, p. 39.

10. For an interesting article on the theme of ascending and descending and its implication for reading the gospel of John as a whole and the story of Nicodemus in particular, cf. Wayne Meeks, "The Man from Heaven in Johannine Sectarianism," in *The Interpretation of John*, John Ashton, ed., Fortress Press, Philadelphia, 1986, pp. 141–173.

11. Karen Horney, *Collected Works of Karen Horney*, Norton Company, N.Y., 1964, p. 85.

12. Carl Gustav Jung, *Memories, Dreams, Reflections*, Anieta Jaffe, ed., Richard and Clara Winston, trans., Random House, N.Y., 1963, p. 252.

13. Rudolf Schnackenburg, *The Gospel According to St. John*, Vol. I, op. cit., p. 370.

14. D. H. Lawrence, *Last Poems*, ed. G. Oriolo, New York, 1933.

15. Elizabeth Bowden Howes, *Intersection and Beyond*, Guild for Psychological Studies, San Francisco, 1971, p. 103.

Chapter 6—John 4:1—4:41

1. H. Van Den Bussche, *The Gospel of the Word*, Priory Press, Chicago, 1967, pp. 53–69.

2. Cf. Raymond Brown, *The Gospel According to John: Volume I*, op. cit., p. 170.

3. Ian T. Ramsey as quoted by R. Alan Culpepper, *Anatomy of the Fourth Gospel: A Study in Literary Design*, op. cit., p. 137.

4. Thomas Kane, *Journey of the Heart: A Way of Praying the Gospels*, St. Bede's Publication, Spencer, 1981, p. 41.

5. Russell Holmes, O.C.D., "A Jungian Approach to Forgetting and Memory," in *St. John of the Cross: Carmelite Studies, Contemporary Psychology and Carmel*, J. Sullivan, ed., I.C.S. Publications, No. 2, Washington, D.C., 1982, pp. 166-219.

6. Adrian Van Kaam, C.S.S.P., *The Woman at the Well*, Dimension Books, Denville, 1976, p. 33.

7. R. Alan Culpepper, *Anatomy of the Fourth Gospel: A Study in Literary Design*, op. cit., p. 192.

Chapter 7—John 5:1—6:1

1. Henri Nouwen, *Reaching Out: Three Movements in the Spiritual Life*, Doubleday, N.Y., 1975, pp. 13-34.

2. John S. Dunne, *Reasons of the Heart: A Journey into Solitude and Back Again into the Human Circle*, op. cit.

3. T. S. Eliot, *Four Quartets*, "East Coker," op. cit., p. 32.

4. Edward Schillebeeckx, *Christ*, op. cit., p. 386.

5. For further discussion on the feasts of Israel and their history, cf. Roland De Vaux, *Ancient Israel*, Vol. 2, McGraw-Hill, N.Y., 1965, pp. 474-483.

6. Raymond Brown, *The Gospel According to John, Volume I*, op. cit., p. 209.

7. William Lynch, *Images of Hope*, op. cit., p. 31.

8. Joan Chittister, O.S.B., *Winds of Change: Women Challenge the Church*, Sheed and Ward, N.Y., 1986, p. 72.

9. William Lynch, *Images of Hope*, op. cit., pp. 159ff.

10. R. Alan Culpepper, *Anatomy of the Fourth Gospel: A Study in Literary Design*, op. cit., p. 127.

11. Robert Kysar, *John the Maverick Gospel*, op. cit., p. 57.

12. John Huckle and Paul Visokay, "The Gospel According to John," op. cit., p. 76.

13. Jerome Neyrey, *Christ Is Community: Christologies of the New Testament*, op. cit., p. 102.

14. Augustine Grady, "Martin Buber and the Gospel of John," *Thought*, Fordham University Quarterly, September 1978, Vol. LIII, No. 210, pp. 283–292.

Chapter 8—John 6:1—7:1

1. For a discussion on the role of "misunderstandings" in John's gospel, cf. R. Alan Culpepper, *Anatomy of the Fourth Gospel: A Study in Literary Design*, op. cit. pp. 152–165.
2. Raymond Brown, "The Ego Eimi Passages in the Fourth Gospel," *Companion to John*, John M. Taylor, ed., Alba House, N.Y., 1977, pp. 117ff. Cf. also Rudolf Schnackenburg, "Origin and Meaning of the Ego Eimi Formula," *The Gospel According to St. John*, Vol. 2, op. cit., pp. 79f.
3. Robert Kysar, "Eschatological Meaning of the I Am Statements," *John the Maverick Gospel*, op. cit., p. 43.
4. Rudolf Schnackenburg, *The Gospel According to St. John*, Vol. 2, op. cit., p. 35.
5. Raymond Brown, "The Ego Eimi Passages in the Fourth Gospel" in *Companion to John*, op. cit., pp. 119–120.
6. Arturo Paoli, *Freedom To Be Free*, Charles Underhill Quinn, trans., Orbis Books, Maryknoll, 1973, p. 182.
7. Ibid., p. 184.
8. Paul Marie De La Croix, O.C.D., *Biblical Spirituality of St. John*, Alba House, N.Y., 1966, p. 330.
9. John Dominic Crossan, "A Structuralist Analysis of John Six in Orientation by Disorientation," *Studies in Literary Criticism* Richard Spenser, ed., Pittsburgh Theological Monograph Series 35, Pickwick Press, 1980, pp. 234–249.
10. Robert Kysar, *The Scandal of Lent*, op. cit., p. 44.
11. Ibid., p. 42.

Chapter 9—John 7:1—8:58

1. The name of the feast itself gives rise to some confusion. Tabernacles is a translation from the word used in the Vulgate that is meaningless. Booths is equally vague. Tents is a literal

translation of the word "tabernacles." In Hebrew the word *sukkoth* is used which is translated as hut, so that the feast is sometimes called the feast of huts. Further and more elaborate information concerning this feast is given in Roland De Vaux, *Ancient Israel*, Vol. 2, op. cit., pp. 495, 502.

2. *Jerome Biblical Commentary*, Vol. 2., op. cit., 100:3:5, p. 439. Cf. also the article previously referred to by W. Meeks on the theme of ascent and descent *(anabanein/katabanein)*. Meeks maintains that "in every instance the motif points to contrast, forgiveness, division and judgment. Only within that dominant structure of estrangement and difference is developed the counterpoint of unity between God and Christ, between God, Christ, and the small group of the faithful." The contrast here then is between Jesus and the disciples: Wayne Meeks, "The Man from Heaven in Johannine Sectarianism," *Interpretation of John*, J. Ashton, ed., op. cit., p. 160.

3. I have adopted and adapted the work of Crossan here in his analysis of John 7—8. Crossan not only sees this section of the gospel as comprised of seven dialogues in reverse parallelism, but he sees the whole gospel of signs developed along similar lines. He submits the following schema:

> (1) 1:19—4:42   (5) 9:1—10:39
> (2) 4:43—5:47   (6) 11:1—11:54
> (3) 6:1—6:71   (7) 12:1—12:36
> (4) 7:1—8:59: this becomes the central section of the gospel book of signs for Crossan, and in turn at the center of this section is 7:45-52. It is therefore the key to the gospel. Cf. John Dominic Crossan, O.S.M., *The Gospel of Eternal Life: Reflections on the Theology of St. John*, op. cit., pp. 86-92.

4. Ibid., p. 86.

5. Raymond Brown, *The Gospel According to John: Volume I*, op. cit., p. 327.

6. H. Van Den Bussche, *The Gospel of the Word*, op. cit., p. 123.

7. R. Alan Culpepper, *Anatomy of the Fourth Gospel: A Study in Literary Design*, op. cit., pp. 146-148. These seven possible responses are taken from Culpepper's work and adapted for my purpose here to the process of decision making.

8. W. H. Auden, "For the Time Being," as quoted in *The Choice Is Always Ours*, Dorothy Phillips, ed., Request Books, Theosophical Publishing House, Wheaton, 1975, p. 77.

Chapter 10—John 8:1—8:12

1. Raymond Brown, *The Gospel According to John: Volume I*, op. cit., p. 325.
2. John Dominic Crossan, O.S.M., *The Gospel of Eternal Life: Reflections on the Theology of St. John*, op. cit., p. 92.
3. Diarmuid McGann, *The Journeying Self: The Gospel of Mark Through a Jungian Perspective*, op. cit., pp. 136ff. Here I deal with the second series of conflict stories in Mark. They occur just before the passion, on the occasion of Jesus' third visit to the temple. I consider them "traps" to snare Jesus. The trapping technique which Mark utilizes lends a note of suspicion, urgency, and violence to the drama of his gospel.
4. Monsignor Coffey was my pastor at St. Patrick's in Bay Shore, New York. I have not quoted him here because I am sharing my recall of his central idea given at a lecture on reconciliation.
5. Richard Gula, S.S., *To Walk Together Again—The Sacrament of Reconciliation*, Paulist Press, N.J., 1984, p. 19.
6. Thomas S. Kane, *Journey of the Heart: A Way of Praying the Gospels*, op. cit., pp. 58–65.
7. The paragraph which follows is a brief summary of the work of Glasser which I have adapted from his article "Conscience and Superego" as it is contained in *Psyche and Spirit*, J. Heaney, ed., Paulist Press, 1973. Cf. also Gula's work, op. cit., pp. 136–186.
8. Elizabeth Bowden Howes, *Man the Choicemaker*, op. cit., p. 195.

Chapter 11—John 9:1—9:41

1. Compare the seven exchanges between Jesus and the woman of Samaria with the seven scenes in this chapter. Compare the

progressive change undergone by both the woman and the blind man as the respective stories unfold.

2. Compare the length of illness of the paralyzed and blind men, the initiative of Jesus, the healing day, the curative power of matter, the intensifying hostility, the confession of faith, etc.

3. Cf. Chapter Two above.

4. Sam Keen, *The Passionate Life: Stages of Loving*, Harper and Row, San Francisco, 1986, p. 136.

5. Dante Aligheri, *The Divine Comedy: Paradiso*, D. Sayers and B. Reynolds, trans., Penguin Books, Baltimore, 1962, p. 145.

6. Tad Dunne, *Lonergan and Spirituality: Toward a Spiritual Integration*, Loyola University Press, Chicago, 1985, p. 17.

7. Sam Keen, *The Passionate Life: Stages of Loving*, op. cit. p. 60.

8. Augustine Grady, S. J., "Martin Buber and the Gospel of John," op. cit., p. 288.

9. T. S. Eliot, *Four Quartets:* "East Coker," op. cit., l. 123.

10. Peter Mann, *Through Words and Images*, CTNA, New York, 1983, pp. 14–15.

11. Carl Gustav Jung, "Archetypes and the Collective Unconscious," *Collected Works*, Vol. 9, p. 217. R.F.C. Hull, trans., Bollinger Series XX, Princeton University Press.

12. R. Alan Culpepper, *Anatomy of the Fourth Gospel: A Study in Literary Design*, op. cit., p. 205.

13. Peter Mann and Diarmuid McGann: notes from a workshop Peter and I gave entitled "Scripture and the Unknown Self." It was suggested there that not only is the self one, protean, multidimensional and mysterious but so also is scripture.

Chapter 12—John 10:1—10:41

1. Cf. Roland De Vaux, *Ancient Israel*, Vol. 2, op. cit., pp. 510–514.

2. Raymond Brown, *The Gospel According to John: Volume I*, op. cit., pp. 388ff.

3. Kenneth Bailey, *Poet and Peasant: A Literary Cultural Approach to the Parables in Luke*, William B. Eerdmans Publishing Co., Michigan, 1976, p. 147.

4. John Painter, *Reading John's Gospel Today,* op. cit., p. 43.
5. Raymond Brown, *The Gospel According to John: Volume I,* op. cit., pp. 404ff.
6. Ibid.
7. Edward Schillebeeckx, *Christ,* op. cit., p. 393.
8. Helen Luke, *Dark Wood to White Rose: A Study of Meanings in Dante's Divine Comedy,* Dove Publications, Pecos, New Mexico, 1975, p. 19.
9. Marion Woodman, *Addiction to Perfection: The Still Unravished Bride,* Inner City Books, Toronto, 1982, p. 13.
10. Ibid., p. 33.

Chapter 13—John 11:1—12:8

1. Cf. Raymond Brown, *The Gospel According to John: Volume I,* op. cit., pp. 430ff.
2. Cf. my comments on chapters 7 and 8 in the gospel as given in Chapter Nine of this book.
3. Crossan suggests the following structure to the chapter:

Dialogue 1	Jesus and Disciples	11:5–16
Dialogue 2	Jesus and Martha	11:17–27
Dialogue 3	Jesus and Mary	11:28–32
Dialogue 4	Jesus and Jews	11:33–37
Dialogue 5	Jesus and Martha	11:38–41
Dialogue 6	Jesus and Father	11:41–42
Dialogue 7	Jesus and Lazarus	11:43–44

Cf. John Dominic Crossan, O.S.M., *The Gospel of Eternal Life: Reflections on the Theology of St. John,* op. cit., p. 101.
4. Elizabeth Bowden Howes, *Jesus' Answer to God,* Guild for Pyschological Studies, San Francisco, 1984, p. 143.
5. Arturo Paoli, *Meditations on Saint Luke,* Bernard William, trans., Orbis Books, Maryknoll, N.Y., 1977, p. 151.
6. Rudolf Schnackenburg, *The Gospel According to St. John,* Vol. 2, op. cit., p. 328.
7. Robert Kysar, *John the Maverick Gospel,* op. cit., p. 85.

8. Elisabeth Schüssler Fiorenza, *In Memory of Her: A Feminist Theological Reconstruction of Christian Origins*, op. cit., p. 329.

9. Ibid., pp. 323–334 for further comment on these.

10. Raymond Brown, *The Gospel According to John: Volume I*, op. cit., p. 435.

11. Rudolf Schnackenburg, *The Gospel According to St. John*, Vol. 2, op. cit., p. 333.

12. Elizabeth Bowden Howes, *Jesus' Answer to God*, op. cit., p. 144.

13. *The Jerome Biblical Commentary*, Vol. 2, op. cit., 63:128, p. 448.

14 Elisabeth Schüssler Fiorenza, *In Memory of Her: A Feminist Theological Reconstruction of Christian Origins*, op. cit., p. 331.

15. R. Alan Culpepper, *Anatomy of the Fourth Gospel: A Study in Literary Design*, op. cit., p. 111.

16. Ibid., p. 142.

17. Fred Culter, *Art and the Wish to Die: An Analysis of Images of Self Injury From Pre-History to the Present*, Chicago, Nelson Hall, 1983, p. 12.

18. W. B. Yeats, *Selected Poetry: Introduction*, A. Norman Jeffries, ed., Pan Books, Macmillan, London, 1974, p. 208.

19. Dylan Thomas, *Collected Poems of Dylan Thomas*, New Directions, N.Y., 1971, p. 128.

20. T. S. Eliot, *Complete Poems and Plays*, "Journey of the Magi," Harcourt Brace and World, N.Y., 1971, pp. 68–69.

Chapter 14—John 13:1—13:31

1. Rudolf Schnackenburg, *The Gospel According to St. John*, Vol. 3, op. cit., p. 109.

2. Raymond Brown, *The Gospel According to John: Volume 2*, op. cit., p. xvii.

3. John Dominic Crossan, *The Gospel of Eternal Life: Reflections on the Theology of St. John*, op. cit., p. 109.

4. Elisabeth Schüssler Fiorenza, *In Memory of Her: A Feminist Theological Reconstruction of Christian Origins*, op. cit., pp. 324–325.

5. R. Alan Culpepper, *Anatomy of the Fourth Gospel: A Study in Literary Design*, op. cit., p. 124.

6. Ibid.
7. Anthony Padovano, *Free To Be Faithful*, Paulist Press, N.J., 1972, p. 91.

Chapter 15—John 13:31—16:31

1. Cf. Raymond Brown, *The Gospel According to John: Volume 2*, op. cit., pp. 597ff.
2. We have previously referred to "misunderstandings" as a pattern in the gospel. For a deeper discussion of this topic, cf. R. Alan Culpepper, *Anatomy of the Fourth Gospel: A Study in Literary Design*, op. cit., pp. 152–165.
3. *Jerome Biblical Commentary*, Vol. 2, op. cit., 63:143:5, p. 453.
4. Augustine Grady, "Martin Buber and the Gospel of John," op. cit., p. 290.
5. R. Alan Culpepper, *Anatomy of the Fourth Gospel: A Study in Literary Design*, op. cit., pp. 152-165.
6. Fernando Segovia, "Peace I Leave with You; My Peace I Give to You: Discipleship in The Fourth Gospel," in *Discipleship in the New Testament*, Fernando Segovia, ed., Fortress Press, Philadelphia, 1985, pp. 76–102.
7. Ibid., p. 87.
8. John Painter, *Reading John's Gospel Today*, op. cit., p. 64.
9. Cf. Robert Kysar, *John the Maverick Gospel*, op. cit., pp. 93ff.
10. Ignace De La Potterie, "The Truth in St. John," in *The Interpretation of John*, J. Ashton, ed., op. cit., p. 61.
11. Raymond Brown, *Gospel*, Vol. 2, Appendix V. p. 1140.
12. Ignace de la Petterie, *The Truth*, op. cit., pp. 53–56.
13. Ibid., p. 60.

Chapter 16—John 17:1—17:24

1. The farewell discourse and the solemn prayer are therefore words of a good shepherd who is there to give his life for his own. To call the prayer high priestly is un-Johannine because the fourth gospel sees Jesus not as high priest but as Mosaic Shepherd. Edward Schillebeeckx, *Christ*, op. cit., p. 401.

2. Elisabeth Kübler Ross, *Death: The Final Stage of Growth*, Prentice-Hall, Englewood Cliffs, N.J., 1975.

3. Raymond Brown, *The Gospel According to John: Volume 2*, op. cit., p. 744.

4. Rudolf Schnackenburg, *The Gospel According to St. John*, Vol. 2, op. cit., p. 399.

5. Philippians 2:1–11.

6. For further development of this, cf. W. K. Grossouw, "Christian Spirituality in John," in *Companion to John*, Michael Taylor, ed., op. cit., p. 212.

7. Cf. J. Louis Martyn, *Glimpses into the History of the Johannine Community: The Gospel of John in Christian History*, op. cit.

8. Jerome Neyrey, S. J., *Christ in Community: Christologies of the New Testament*, op. cit., pp. 176ff.

9. John Sheets, S. J., *The Spirit Speaks in Us*, Dimension Books, N.J., 1969, pp. 59–67.

10. Ibid., p. 60.

11. Raymond Brown, *The Gospel According to John: Volume 2*, op. cit., p. 776.

12. This particular aspect of the thought of Teilhard De Chardin has been pursued and developed by Ursula King, *Toward a New Mysticism—Teilhard De Chardin and Eastern Religions*, Seabury, N.Y., 1980. For the reader more interested in reading Teilhard's own thoughts in this direction the following works are recommended: *Human Energy* (1969), *Activation of Energy* (1970), *Christianity and Evolution* (1971), all published by Harper and Row.

13. Erich Neumann, *The Origins and History of Consciousness*, Bollingen Series, XLII, Princeton University Press, 1954.

14. Carl Gustav Jung, *Collected Works*, esp. Vol. 6 and 9, Bollingen Series XX, Princeton University Press.

Chapter 17—John 18:1—19:42

1. Compare Mark 14:32ff.

2. For a further discussion of John's use of irony in the fourth

gospel, cf. R. Alan Culpepper, *Anatomy of the Fourth Gospel: A Study in Literary Design,* op. cit., pp. 165ff.

3. John Dominic Crossan, *The Gospel of Eternal Life: Reflections on the Theology of St. John,* op. cit., p. 122.
4. Ibid.
5. Culpepper, op. cit., p. 143.
6. For a discussion of the praetorium, Lithostroton and Gabbatha, cf. Pierre Benoit, *Jesus and the Gospels,* Benet Weetherhead, trans., Herder and Herder, N.Y., 1973, pp. 166–188.
7. D. Moody Smith, "The Presentation of Jesus in the Fourth Gospel," *Interpreting the Gospel,* J. Luther Mays, ed., Fortress Press, 1981, p. 282.
8. Pierre Benoit, *The Passion and Resurrection of Jesus Christ,* Benet Weetherhead, trans., Herder and Herder, N.Y., 1970, p. 149.
9. Josef Blank, "The Gospel According to John," *New Testament for Spiritual Reading,* No. 9, Vol. 3, John McKenzie, ed., Crossroad, N.Y., 1981, p. 62.
10. Ernst Kasemann, "Toward the Interpretation of John's Gospel: A Discussion of the Testament of Jesus" by Ernst Kasemann; Gunther Bornkamm in *The Interpreting John,* J. Ashton, ed., op. cit., pp. 79–94.
11. Robert Kysar, *The Scandal of Lent,* op. cit., p. 91.
12. Elisabeth Schüssler Fiorenza, *In Memory of Her: A Feminist Theological Reconstruction of Christian Origins,* op. cit., p. 331.
13. W. B. Yeats, "The Second Coming," *W. B. Yeats Selected Poetry,* A. Norman Jeffares, ed., op. cit., p. 99.
14. Henri Nouwen, "Living in Joyful Ecstasy," articles in *Sojourners* Aug./Sept. 1985, p. 27.

Chapter 18—John 20:1—20:20

1. Edward Schillebeeckx, *Christ,* op. cit., p. 419.
2. Ibid., p. 417.
3. Ibid.
4. Josef Blank, "The Gospel According to John," *New Testament for Spiritual Reading,* op. cit., p. 128.

5. Fernando Segovia, "Discipleship in the Fourth Gospel," in *Discipleship in the New Testament,* op. cit., p. 101, footnote 62.
6. I have selected these three tenses from an article in *Share the Word,* Paulist Fathers, Washington, D.C., March/April 1985. The three categories they refer to are Before, After and Ever Afterwards.
7. Cf. chapters 7 and 8 in John's Gospel and our Chapter 9 above where we suggest that choice in a liturgical context is the central focus of these chapters.
8. Fernando Segovia, "Discipleship in the Fourth Gospel," in *Discipleship in the New Testament,* op. cit., p. 101, footnote 61.
9. Robert Kysar, *The Scandal of Lent,* op. cit., p. 101.
10. Josef Blank, "The Gospel According to John," *New Testament for Spiritual Reading,* op. cit., p. 139.
11. Paul Ricoeur, *Freud and Philosophy: An Essay on Interpretation,* Yale University Press, New Haven, 1970.
12. Tad Dunne, S.J., *Lonergan and Spirituality: Toward a Spiritual Integration,* op. cit., p. 183.
13. Ibid.

Chapter 19—John 21:1—21:24

1. Schnackenburg offers the following critique of some of these: "None of these designations fully applies. It is not a postscript because there is nothing more to be said; appendix is to see it too much from an external point of view not corresponding to the inner importance given to the chapter by the editors; epilogue sounds (at least in German) again too inconsiderable to be just in respect of the function intended for it. It is an ultimate editorial chapter having an explanatory function for the readers in the church of those days." Rudolf Schnackenburg, *The Gospel According to St. John,* Vol. 3, op. cit., p. 344.
2. Josef Blank, "The Gospel According to John," Vol. 3, op. cit., p. 146.
3. Luke 24:13.
4. Raymond Brown, Karl Donfried, John Reumann, eds., *Peter in*

the New Testament: A Collaborative Assessment by Protestant and Roman Catholic Scholars, Augsburg Publishing House, Minneapolis and Paulist Press, New York, 1973, p. 143.

5. Rudolf Schnackenburg, *The Gospel According to St. John*, Vol. 3, op. cit., p. 359.

6. Ceslaus Spicq, O.P., "Agape in the New Testament," Vol. 3, *Agape in Saint John*, Sister Marie Aquinas McNamara, O.P. and Sister Mary Honorie Richter, O.P., trans., Herder Book Co., Missouri, 1966, p. 96.

7. Ibid., p. 88.

8. Raymond Brown, Karl Donfried, John Reumann, *Peter in the New Testament: A Collaborative Assessment by Protestant and Roman Catholic Scholars*, op. cit., pp. 142ff.

9. Ibid., p. 144.

10. Rudolf Schnackenburg, *The Gospel According to St. John*, Vol. 3, op. cit., p. 375.

11. R. Alan Culpepper, *Anatomy of the Fourth Gospel: A Study in Literary Design*, op. cit., p. 14.

12. Rudolf Schnackenburg, *The Gospel According to St. John*, Vol. 3, op. cit., p. 368.

13. Josef Blank, "The Gospel According to John," Vol. 3, op. cit., p. 155.

14. Elizabeth Bowden Howes, *Jesus' Answer to God*, op. cit., p. 27.